Student Resource Manual

to accompany

FOURTH EDITION

SOCIOLOGY

IN A CHANGING WORLD

prepared by

WILLIAM KORNBLUM

and

CAROLYN D. SMITH

HARCOURT BRACE COLLEGE PUBLISHERS

Fort Worth Philadelphia San Diego New York Orlando Austin San Antonio
Toronto Montreal London Sydney Tokyo

Requests for permission to make copies of any part of the work should be mailed to:
Permissions Department, Harcourt Brace & Company, 6277 Sea Harbor Drive, Orlando, FL 32887-6777.

Address for Editorial Correspondence
Harcourt Brace College Publishers, 301 Commerce Street, Suite 3700, Fort Worth, TX 76102

Address for Orders
Harcourt Brace & Company, 6277 Sea Harbor Drive, Orlando, FL 32887
1-800-782-4479

ISBN: 0-15-504005-7

Printed in the United States of America

7 8 9 0 1 2 3 4 5 6   066   10 9 8 7 6 5 4 3 2

PREFACE

Welcome, social explorer. You must be one of the more inquisitive ones—after all, you are taking the time to read this supplement to your text. We hope this manual will provide you with some stimulating and practical applications of your sociological knowledge.

In the shadowy time of early human history, people believed in supernatural spirits and the use of spells. The courageous world traveler was often given some talisman or magical potion to ward off dangers, imaginary and real. In sociology we have no magical weapons or potions. But as you begin voyaging through the worlds of strangers, in your own and other societies, there are sociological concepts and methods that are far more powerful than a spell or charm. Knowledge about social power, bureaucracy, the dynamics of interaction in small groups, the basics of what makes cultures operate—these and many other sociolgical insights can help you negotiate your way through the risks and mysteries of new societies, new communities, or new organizations. Sociological concepts and the development of your sociological imagination can also help you gain greater insight into the workings of your own familiar social environment.

This resource manual presents three different types of assistance to the sociological voyager. First, the manual presents some of the basic rules for crafting a sociological research paper, including a concise description of the way sociological materials should be referred to in your papers and research exercises. Second, there is a guide to some of the sociological resources now available on the World Wide Web. These sites encourage you to embark on an almost endless trip through the many sociological projects under way around the world. Finally, there is a set of readings that are referred to in the text but are not presented there in their original form.

DOCUMENTING YOUR RESEARCH

The first section of this manual is somewhat mundane but useful nonetheless to the sociological voyager. If you desire to develop your sociological background or to gain social science credentials (social work, psychology, law, economics, and so on), you'll have to master the basics of scholarly writing. This means library research, footnotes, contruction of bibliographies, and the like. After you become familiar with the basic style of citations, the real work of finding sources and discovering unexpected research treasures awaits you. Don't let the dry qualities of scholarly research blind you to the exciting possibilities of discovery.

EXPLORING SOCIOLOGY
ON THE WORLD WIDE WEB

If you have access to a computer with a Web browser, you can use some of the addresses offered in this manual to do a great deal of original sociological exploration. The addresses we have provided are only the very beginning of what is currently available. The section assumes that you have some familiarity with browsing the Web and are equipped to do so. If this is not the case, you should consider paying a visit to your college computer center or local public library. There you will be able to get some of the basic training necessary to access the Web addresses mentioned in this manual.

There are sociologists and other social scientists all over the world who are busy posting information on the Web. From the addresses we have provided it will be possible to branch out to a large number of other sites that describe fascinating research and opportunities to get involved.

It is also possible to learn a great deal about sociological careers on the Web. Any of the universities with graduate programs in sociology will be glad to send you e-mail about their programs, as will the major professional associations listed here. Once you have learned about a program or a school on the Web, it is usually possible to send an e-mail request for more information, applications, or other materials. And this is true not only of places in the United States but also for programs and projects all over the world. Sociology, in fact, is one of the fields that has helped create the World Wide Web.

THE READINGS

Sociology in a Changing World presents basic definitions of sociological concepts and examples of sociological research that incorporates those concepts. We briefly describe the seminal contributions of many sociologists. This supplement presents some examples of actual papers that are referred to in the text. By reading these papers, you get a sense of how the various sociologists (or sociologically informed authors) actually write and develop their thoughts. Reading the original versions will help you develop your own sociological imagination.

The readings are grouped according to the main parts of the text. They are a combination of classic articles by authors whose work is always cited in sociology and more recent works by authors whose research addresses the most pressing issues of our time. W. E. B. Dubois's outstanding essay on the origins of freedom is an example of sociological theory in action, while Claire Sterk's research on AIDS and prostitution is a model of applied qualitative research. Erving Goffman's essay on stigma and social identity is an example of theoretical writing from the symbolic interactionist perspective, while Portes and Rumbaut, two of the most respected scholars on immigration issues, deal with empirical matters concerning a contemporary population trend.

To discuss social divisions, we offer three strong essays, each highlighting a different form of sociological thought. C. W. Mills's description of the influence of the "corporate rich" is an outstanding example of critical sociology; British sociologist Peter Townsend's essay on the changing world map of poverty is an example of empirical demographic work by a highly committed scholar; and Cynthia Fuchs Epstein's essay on gender and work is an example of strong functionalist analysis of how work structures bear differently on the careers of men and women.

Finally, we have included three essays concerning social institutions. George Orwell's classic and ironic essay on how language is subverted by people in power, Nancy Tatom Ammerman's empirical analysis of divisions in a major religious denomination, and Andrew Cherlin's discussion of divorce and remarriage provide opportunities for you to read at greater length some of the original sources presented in the text itself. We hope you will do so and can assure you that your time will be well spent.

Each part of this manual offers some keys to sociological insight. None can do magic, but all can lead you down some new paths where only you can discover what kind of opportunities will reward your efforts.

CONTENTS

Guidelines for
Research and Documentation

Guidelines for Research and Documentation

Library research is an important component of research in the social sciences. Only after the researcher has developed a sufficient foundation for the study through library research can he or she pursue data collection through interviews, questionnaires, and field observations. Social scientists survey attitudes, record responses, and interview subjects to obtain reliable evidence. Many of their data are numerical, reported in tables and charts. It is essential for social scientists to know how to read and interpret such figures so that they can analyze data and develop conclusions. Much of your library research in social science disciplines will depend on abstracting information from such tables and charts. Therefore, general reference sources like government yearbooks and almanacs may be particularly useful.

GENERAL LIBRARY SOURCES

The following list is a guide to some of the major sources—indexes, encyclopedias, bibliographies, and other library materials—that you can use to find general research information.

INDEXES
Biography Index
Government Documents Index
Magazine Index
New York Times Index
Public Affairs Information Services Index
Reader's Guide to Periodical Literature
Wall Street Journal Index
Washington Post Index

ENCYCLOPEDIAS
Academic American Encyclopedia
Encyclopedia Americana
Encyclopaedia Brittanica
    Micropaedia
    Propaedia
The New Columbia Encyclopedia
The Random House Encyclopedia

BIBLIOGRAPHIES
Books in Print
The Bibliographic Index

The Subject Guide to Books in Print
Paperbound Books in Print

OTHER SOURCES

Dissertation Abstracts International
Editorials on File
Monthly Catalog of United States Government Publications
Historical Atlas
Encyclopaedia Brittanica World Atlas
Facts on File
Statistical Abstracts
World Almanac

GENERAL DATABASES
FOR COMPUTER SEARCHES

In many cases computerized searching makes research much faster and provides the option of combining key words (or *descriptors*) with author and title information to find exact citations. For instance, you may know only that Fredric Jameson has written an article on third-world literature, but not where it has been published or the exact title or contents. Since the article is about literature, you decide to search a literature database, which yields various titles by Fredric Jameson. Matching the titles found with the key words "Third-world Literature," you find the following: Jameson, Fredric, "World Literature in an Age of Multinational Capitalism," in *The Current in Criticism* edited by Clayton Koelb and Virgil Lokke.

Some of the most widely used general databases include the *Magazine Index, Dissertation Abstracts Online, Biography Index, Books in Print, GPO Monthly Catalog, Newsearch, National Newspaper Index, New York Times Index, Marquis Who's Who,* and the *Reader's Guide to Periodical Literature.*

It is important to remember that although many databases have a print counterpart, some are available only on-line.

CD-ROM is a rapidly expanding new technology for database searching which is available in many libraries. Many indexes that are available in a print version are now offered on CD-ROM. CD-ROM offers a cost savings over on-line database searching and more flexibility than searching print indexes.

SPECIALIZED LIBRARY SOURCES

The following reference sources are useful in a variety of social science disciplines.

ASI Index (American Statistics Institute)
Encyclopedia of Black America
Handbook of North American Indians
Human Resources Abstracts
International Bibliography of the Social Sciences
International Encyclopedia of the Social Sciences
PAIS Public Affairs Information Service
Population Index
Social Sciences Citation Index

The following reference sources are most often used for research in specific disciplines.

Anthropology
Abstracts in Anthropology
Anthropological Index

Business and Economics
Business Periodicals Index

Criminal Justice
Abstracts on Criminology and Penology
Abstracts on Police Science
Criminal Justice Abstracts
Criminal Justice Periodicals Index

Education
Dictionary of Education
Education Index
Encyclopedia of Educational Research

Political Science
ABC Political Science
CIS Index (Congressional Information Service)
Combined Retrospective Index to Journals in Political Science
Encyclopedia of Modern World Politics
Encyclopedia of the Third World
Foreign Affairs Bibliography
Information Services on Latin America
International Political Science Abstracts
United States Political Science Documents
U.S. Serial Set Index

Psychology
Author Index to Psychological Index and Psychological Abstracts
Contemporary Psychology
Cumulative Subject Index to Psychological Abstracts
Encyclopedia of Psychology
Psychological Abstracts

Sociology
Poverty and Human Resources Abstracts
Rural Sociology Abstracts
Sage Family Studies Abstracts
Sociological Abstracts

GOVERNMENT DOCUMENTS

Government documents are important resources for social scientists. They contain the most complete and up-to-date facts and figures necessary for any social analysis. Varied information—from technical, scientific, and medical information to everyday information on home safety for children—can be found in government documents.

Government documents can be searched through the *Monthly Catalog,* which contains the list of documents published that month together with a subject index. Other indexes include *The Congressional Information Service Index, The American Statistics Index,* and *The Index to U.S. Government Periodicals.*

NEWSPAPER ARTICLES

Newspaper articles are particularly useful sources for researching subjects in political science, history, economics, or social work. Students usually rely on the *New York Times,* which has indexes available both in print and on microfilm. However, for newspaper information from across the country, a handy and useful source is *Newsbank. Newsbank,* like the government's *Monthly Catalog,* provides subject headings under the appropriate government agencies. For instance, articles on child abuse are likely to be listed under Health and Human Services. Older articles will be listed in older *Newsbanks* under Health, Education, and Welfare. Once you find the subject area, *Newsbank* provides a microcard/microfiche number. On that microfiche, you will find articles from around the country on your subject.

SPECIALIZED DATABASES FOR COMPUTER SEARCHES

Many of the print sources cited above have electronic counterparts. Some of the more widely used databases for social science disciplines include *Cendata, Business Periodicals Index, PsycINFO, ERIC, Social Scisearch, Sociological Abstracts, Information Science Abstracts, PAIS International, Population Bibliography, Economic Literature Index, BI/INFORM, Legal Resources Index, Management Contents, Trade and Industry Index,* and *PTS F+S Indexes.*

NON-LIBRARY SOURCES

Interviews, questionnaires, surveys, and observation of the behavior of various groups and individuals are some of the important non-library sources in social science research. Sometimes students conduct these types of research themselves. Sometimes professors provide unpublished results from these types of research that have been conducted by other students, the professor, colleagues of the professor, institutions, agencies, or research contractors. Assignments given by your professor may ask you to use your classmates as subjects for questionnaires. In political science, your teacher may ask you to interview a sample of college students and classify them as conservative, liberal, or radical. You may be asked to poll each group to find out college students' attitudes on nuclear energy, chemical waste disposal, the homeless, and other issues that affect them. If you were writing a paper on educational programs for gifted students, in addition to library research on the issue, you might want to observe two classes—one of gifted students and one of students not participating in the gifted program. You may also want to interview students, teachers, or parents. In psychology and social work, your research may rely on the observations of clients and patients and be written up as a case study.

Documenting Sources

Documentation is the acknowledgment of what you have derived from a source and exactly where in that source you found your material. Not all fields use the same style of documentation. The most widely used formats are those advocated by the Modern Language Association (MLA), *The Chicago Manual of Style* (CMS), and the American Psychological Association (APA). In addition, the sciences, engineering, and medicine have their own formats. Before writing a paper in any of these areas, you should ask your instructor what style of documentation you should use and then follow it consistently throughout your paper.

WHAT TO DOCUMENT

You must document all materials that you borrow from your sources. Documentation enables your readers to identify your sources and to judge the quality of your work. It also encourages them to look up the books and articles that you cite. Therefore, you should carefully document the following kinds of information:

1. direct quotations
2. summaries or paraphrases of material from your sources
3. opinions, judgments, and original insights of others
4. illustrations, tables, graphs, and charts that you get from your sources

The references in your text should clearly point a reader to the borrowed material and should clearly differentiate your ideas from the ideas of your sources.

WHAT NOT TO DOCUMENT

Common knowledge, information that you would expect most educated readers to know, need not be documented. You can assume, for instance, that undocumented information that appears in several sources is generally known. You can also safely include facts that are widely used in encyclopedias, textbooks, newspapers, and magazines, or on television and radio. Even if the information is new to you, as long as it is generally accepted as fact, you need not indicate your source. However, information that is in dispute or that is credited to a particular person should be documented. You need not, for example, document the fact that the Declaration of Independence was signed on July 4, 1776, or that Josiah Bartlett and Oliver Wolcott signed it. However, you do have to document a historian's analysis of the document, or a particular scholar's recent discoveries about Josiah Bartlett.

As you can see, when to document is sometimes a matter of judgment. As a beginning researcher, you should document any material you believe might need acknowledgment, even if you suspect it might be common knowledge. By doing so, you avoid the possibility of plagiarism.

Documentation Format

Documentation format in the social sciences is more uniform than in the humanities or the sciences. The disciplines and journals in the social sciences almost uniformly use the documentation style of the American Psychological Association's *Publication Manual.*

THE APA FORMAT*

APA format, which is used extensively in the social sciences, relies on short references—consisting of the last name of the author and the year of publication—inserted within the text. These references are keyed to an alphabetical list of references that follows the paper.

*APA documentation format follows the guidelines set in the *Publication Manual of the American Psychological Association.* 4th ed. Washington, DC: APA, 1994.

Parenthetical References in the Text

One author.   The APA format calls for a comma between the name and the date, whereas MLA format does not.

> One study of stress in the workplace (Weisberg, 1985) shows a correlation between . . .

You should not include in the parenthetical reference information that appears in the text.

> In his study, Weisberg (1983) shows a correlation . . .
> (author's name in text)

> In Weisberg's 1983 study of stress in the workplace . . .
> (author's name and date in text)

Two publications by the same author(s), same year.   If you cite two or more publications by the same author that appeared the same year, the first is designated *a*, the second *b* (e.g., Weisberg, 1983a; Weisberg, 1983b), and so on. These letter designations also appear in the reference list that follows the text of your paper.

> He completed his next study of stress (Weisberg, 1983b). . . .

A publication by two or more authors.   When a work has two authors, both names are cited every time you refer to it.

> There is a current and growing concern over the use of psychological testing in elementary schools (Albright & Glennon, 1982).

If a work has three, four, or five authors, mention all names in the first reference, and in subsequent references cite the first author followed by *et al.* and the year (Sparks et al., 1984). When a work has six or more authors, cite the name of the first author followed by *et al.* and the year in first and subsequent references.

When citing multiple authors in the text of your paper, join the names of the last two with *and* (According to Rosen, Wolfe, and Ziff [1988] . . .). In parenthetical documentation, however, use an ampersand to join multiple authors (Rosen, Wolfe, & Ziff, 1988).

Specific parts of a source.   When citing a specific part of a source, you should identify that part in your reference. APA documentation includes abbreviations for the words *page* ("p."), *chapter* ("chap."), and *section* ("sec.").

> These theories have an interesting history (Lee, 1966, p. 53).

Two or more works within the same parenthetical reference.   List works by different authors in alphabetical order. Separate items with a semicolon.

> . . . among several studies (Barson & Roth, 1985; Rose, 1987; Tedesco, 1982).

List works by the same author in order of date of publication.

> . . . among several studies (Weiss & Elliot, 1982, 1984, 1985).

Distinguish works by the same author that appeared in the same year by designating the first *a*, the second *b*, and so on. (*In press* designates a work about to be published.)

> . . . among several studies (Hossack, 1985a, 1985b, 1985c, in press).

Quotation. For a quotation, a page number appears in addition to the author's name and the year.

> Because of information about Japanese success, the United States has come to realize that "Japanese productivity has successfully challenged, even humiliated, America in world competition" (Bowman, 1984, p. 197).

The page number for a long quotation (40 words or more) also appears in parentheses but follows the period that ends the last sentence.

> As Rehder (1983) points out,
> Here women receive low wages, little job security, and less opportunity for training or educational development. . . . (p. 43)

LISTING THE REFERENCES

The list of all the sources cited in your paper falls at the end on a new numbered page with the heading *References.*

Items are arranged in alphabetical order, with the author's last name spelled out in full and initials only for the author's first and second names. Next comes the date of publication, title, and, for journal entries, volume number and pages. For books, the date of publication, city of publication, and publisher are included. Indent the first line of each entry five to seven spaces. Begin subsequent lines at the left margin.* Double space within and between entries.

- In the reference list

  Last name   Initials   Date   Underlined title (only first word capitalized)   City   Publisher
  ↓   ↓   ↓   ↓   ↓   ↓
  Morgan, C. T. (1986). Introduction to psychology. New York: Knopf.

  When determining the order of works in the reference list, keep the following guidelines in mind.

- Single-author entries precede multiple-author entries that begin with the same name.

  Field, S. (1987) . . .

  Field, S., & Levitt, M. P. (1984) . . .

- Entries by the same author or authors are arranged according to the year of publication, starting with the earliest date.

  Ruthenberg, H., & Rubin, R. (1985) . . .

  Ruthenberg, H., & Rubin, R. (1987) . . .

- Entries having the same author and date of publication are arranged alphabetically according to title. They include lowercase letters after the year.

  Wolk, E. M. (1986a). Analysis . . .

  Wolk, E. M. (1986b). Hormonal . . .

---

*The APA recommends this format for all manuscripts submitted for publication. If your instructor prefers, you may instead type the first line of each entry flush with the left margin and indent subsequent lines three spaces.

Sample Citations: Books

Capitalize only the first word of the title and the first word of the subtitle of books. Be sure to underline the title and to enclose in parentheses the date, volume number, and edition number. Separate major divisions of each entry with a period and one space.

A book with one author.

Maslow, A. H. (1974). <u>Toward a psychology of being.</u> Princeton: Van Nostrand.

A book with more than one author.   Notice that both authors are cited with last names first.

Blood, R. O., & Wolf, D. M. (1960). <u>Husbands and wives: The dynamics of married living.</u> Glencoe: Free Press.

An edited book.

Lewin, K., Lippitt, R., & White, R. K. (Eds.). (1985). <u>Social learning and imitation.</u> New York: Basic Books.

A work in more than one volume.

Jones, P. R., & Williams, T. C. (Eds). (1990–1993). <u>Handbook of therapy</u> (Vols. 1–2). Princeton: Princeton University Press.

Note: The parenthetical citation in the text would be (Jones & Williams, 1990–1993).

A later edition.

Boshes, L. D., & Gibbs, F. A. (1972). <u>Epilepsy handbook</u> (2nd ed.). Springfield, IL: Thomas.

A book with a corporate author.

League of Women Voters of the United States. (1969). <u>Local league handbook.</u> Washington, DC: Author.

A book review.   Place material that describes the form or content of the reference—review, interview, and so on—within brackets.

Nagle, J. H. (1970). The consumer view of advertising in America [Review of <u>Advertising in America: The consumer view</u>] <u>Personal Psychology 23,</u> 133–134.

A translated book.

Carpentier, A. (1976). <u>Reasons of state.</u> (F. Partridge, Trans.). New York: W. W. Norton.

Sample Citations: Articles

Capitalize only the first word of the title and the first word of the subtitle of articles. Do not underline the article or enclose it in quotation marks. Give the journal title in full; underline the title and capitalize all major words. Underline the volume number and include the issue number in parentheses. Give inclusive page numbers. Separate major divisions of each entry with a period and one space.

An article in a scholarly journal with continuous pagination through an annual volume.

Miller, W. (1969). Violent crimes in city gangs. <u>Journal of Social Issues 27,</u> 581–593.

An article in a scholarly journal that has separate pagination in each issue.

Williams, S., & Cohen, L. R. (1984). Child stress in early learning situations. <u>American Psychologist, 21</u> (10), 1–28.

An encyclopedia article.

Hodge, R. W., & Siegel, P. M. (1968). The measurement of social class. In D. L. Sills (Ed.), <u>International Encyclopedia of the Social Sciences</u> (Vol. 15, pp. 316–324). New York: Macmillan.

A magazine article.

Note: Use *p.* or *pp.* when referring to page numbers in magazines or newspapers *without* volume numbers. Omit the abbreviation for page numbers in referring to publications *with* volume numbers.

Miller, G. A. (1984, November). The test: Alfred Binet's method of identifying subnormal children. <u>Science,</u> pp. 55–57.

Hadingham, E. (1994, April). The mummies of Xinjiang. <u>Discover, 15</u> (4), 68–77.

A newspaper article.

Study finds many street people mentally ill. (1984, June 10). <u>New York Times,</u> p. A7.

Boffy, P. M. (1982, January 24). Security and science collide on data flow. <u>New York Times,</u> p. A20.

An article in an edited book.

Tappan, P. W. (1980). Who is a criminal? In M. E. Wolfgang, L. Savitz, & N. Johnston (Eds.), <u>The sociology of crime and delinquency</u> (pp. 41–48). New York: Wiley.

A government publication.

National Institute of Mental Health. (1985). Television and the family: A
report on the effect on children of violence and family television viewing (DHHS
Publication No. ADM 851274). Washington, DC: U.S. Government Printing Office.

An abstract.

Pippard, J., & Ellam, L. (1981). Electro-convulsive treatment in Great
Britain. <u>British Journal of Psychiatry, 139,</u> 563–568. (From <u>Psychological
Abstracts,</u> 1982, <u>68,</u> Abstract No. 1567)

An interview.

Anderson, A., & Southern, T. (1958). [Interview with Nelson Algren]. In
M. Cowley (Ed.), <u>Writers at work</u> (pp. 231–249). New York: Viking.

If the interview is not published, it does not appear in "References." Instead, the text of the paper should clarify
the interview's nature and date. The same applies to other personal communications, including letters and
electronic messages.

Non-print Sources

A film or videotape.

Kramer, S. (Producer), & Benedek, L. (Director). (1951). <u>Death of a
salesman</u> [Film]. Burbank: Columbia.

Electronic media.   APA recommends the following generic formats for referring to on-line information:

Author, I. (date). Title of article. <u>Title of Periodical</u> [On-line], xx. Available:
Specific path

Author, I. (date). Title of article. [CD-ROM]. <u>Title of Journal,</u> xx, xxx–xxx.
Abstract from: Source and retrieval number.

Sociology on the Internet

There is a substantial amount of sociological information available on the Internet. In fact, many sociologists use the Internet extensively to post their recent research and to correspond with groups of other researchers and interested people who share their particular concerns or research goals. Whenever you are working on a sociological research paper or wondering what some of the latest developments in an area of sociological research might be, it is rather easy to find answers to your questions on the Internet. And since so much of what governments do to create social policy draws on sociological research, public agencies provide large amounts of information about social issues on the Internet.

All you need to begin exploring sociological issues on the Internet is a computer equipped with a modem, and access to an Internet Web browser. Major Internet providers like America Online (AOL), CompuServe, or Prodigy will be happy to hook you up to the Internet from your home, for a monthly fee. Or, if you wish a potentially cheaper service with fewer frills and commercial connections, you can access information about many of them at this Web address: http://www.celestin.com/pocoa/domestic/d_rega.html.

You also no doubt can gain access to the Internet though your college or university or through your local public library. Eventually, however, if you get hooked on browsing the World Wide Web and using other Internet features, you will want your own computer and Internet provider so you can reach into this world of information and services at your convenience.

Another reason for getting on the Internet is the access it affords to library resources. The catalog of almost every major library in the world is now accessible on the Internet. This means you can look up sources that might not be available in your local library. Unfortunately, it does not mean you can actually get your hands on them. Once you have found something you want, however, you will be able to get the complete citation and possibly order it through interlibrary loan. Ask your reference librarian about this invaluable service. It can be especially useful for locating those unique books that are available only in far-off places. But even knowing about the existence of library sources, and their correct citations, can be a great aid in doing a research paper.

You can research almost any topic on the Internet. We will show you some of the basic ways to begin searching through sociological pages on the World Wide Web. There are also innumerable sociology discussion groups elsewhere on the Internet, but the Web alone has so much that we will confine this discussion to that rich resource. All of the Web pages we mention not only lead to other possibilities but also include the names of sociologists or other experts who invite you to send e-mail to them for further communication.

In addition to research materials, you can find all the information you would want about careers in sociology, from graduate schools and research positions to careers in which sociological insights are applied on the job. You can find out about undergraduate and graduate programs in sociology, and many of the universities and colleges you might access will offer suggestions about additional Internet resources in sociology.

The following discussion of sociology on the Internet is based on the major parts of the textbook, beginning with an introduction to sociology and proceeding to more specific subject areas.

Introduction to Sociology on the Internet

If you type in "Social Science: Sociology" on *Yahoo* (*www.Yahoo.com*), one of the most powerful and most frequently used search engines on the Internet, your search will come up with a page that offers a great many options, including sociological organizations, journals, institutes, and a number of other choices. All of these choices will lead you to additional Web pages. Some of them may be extremely helpful; others may be interesting but not what you are looking for. But if you write in the search box "American Sociological Associa-tion" you cannot go wrong. This will bring up the Web page of the national sociology association, shown here.

   Every underlined entry is interactive, which means that when you move the arrow to it using your mouse, a hand appears that notifies you that you can click onto this Web site from the American Sociological Association page. Now click on the box marked "Sections." This will take you to a list of all the special research sections of the American Sociological Association.

American Sociological Association

- Serving Sociologists in Their Work
- Advancing Sociology as a Science and Profession
- Promoting the Contributions and Use of Sociology to Society

What's New—December 19, 1996

You are invited to browse the following new topics:

- ASA's on-line issue of the **Employment Bulletin (January 1997),** our monthly publication of employment listings and fellowship opportunities
- **Funding Opportunities** at the American Sociological Association
- **1996 ASA Awards recipients**
- **Information on 1997 ASA Membership: application, renewals, and benefits**
- **1997 Annual Meeting Call for Papers**
- **1998 Annual Meeting** theme and invitation for suggestions.

Other topics of interest:

New ASA publications:

Social Causes of Violence: Crafting a Science Agenda

Style Guide

1996 Guide to Graduate Departments

Directory of Sociologists in Policy and Practice

● ●

About ASA

ASA Code of Ethics

Membership Information

Meetings & Conferences

Publications

Sections

Governance/Committees

Coming soon:

- Selected stories from *Footnotes,* ASA's newsletter
- Information on sociology for the general public

You can reach us by e-mail at: executive.office@asanet.org

The next page that comes up will offer a list of all the Research Sections officially recognized and supported by the American Sociological Association. Here is almost every conceivable research interest that you might have, and much more. Suppose, for example, that you are interested in social change and social movements that may bring about social change. Click on the interactive line that says "Section on Collective Behavior and Social Movements" and you will see the following Web page.

This site is best viewed with Netscape Navigator. If you are having problems they likely will be solved if you switch to Netscape. Click the Icon to Download. If you continue to have problems, please see the help file.

Section on Collective Behavior and Social Movements

The Section | Resources | Call for Papers |

Welcome to the Home Page of the American Sociological Association Section on Collective Behavior and Social Movements.

The purpose of the CBSM section is to foster the study of emergent and extra-institutional social forms and behavior, particularly crowds and social movements. This includes but is not limited to disasters, riots, protests, rumors, panics, fads, fashions, popular culture, strikes, and reform, revival and revolutionary movements.

CBSM Section Information

➤ **About the CBSM Section and How to Join.**

➤ **Electronic Directory of Members.** Contact other CBSM scholars and add your own entry on-line.

➤ **Current Section Officers.**

➤ **Current Contents of the *Critical Mass Bulletin.*** The CBSM Section's official newsletter

➤ **Section By-Laws.**

Resources of Interest to CBSM Members

➤ **CBSM Teaching Resources** *New and Improved!*

➤ **Activism on the Web** contains a categorized list of links to activist and politically oriented web and gopher pages. Content ranges widely across issues and the political spectrum.

➤ **Sociology Department Web Pages** provides a current listing of sociology department Web Pages in North America and provides links to lists of sociology departments world-wide.

Professional Organizations (Sociology and related fields)

➤ **The American Sociological Association**

➤ **ASA Section on Methods**

➤ **ASA Section on Culture**

➤ **ASA Section on Organizations, Occupations, and Work**

➤ **The International Sociological Association**

➤ **The European Sociological Association**

➤ **Mid-South Sociological Association**

➤ **SSS Southern Sociological Society**

➤ **North Central Sociological Association**

➤ **Sociological Methodology**

➤ **Annual Review—Sociology Online**

➤ **American Psychological Association PsychNET**

➤ **Peace Studies Association**

➤ **Society for the Study of Symbolic Interaction**

➤ **International Network for Social Network Analysis**

➤ **Social Science Computing Association**

➤ **The Center for the Study of Group Processes**

Miscellaneous Sociology Resources on the Web

➤ **SocioWeb**

Calls for Papers and Participation

➤ **1997 Annual Meeting of the American Sociological Association**

➤ **Sociological Perspectives: Special Issue**

➤ **Announcements: Need Information**

This page is maintained by Dan Myers through the Department of Sociology at the University of Wisconsin—Madison. If you have feedback about this homepage please send mail to myers@ssc.wisc.edu.

Last updated on 11/1/96. Netscape enhanced.

Each of the organizations listed on this Web site will lead you to more resources and materials that you might use for research papers, career advice, information about social action, and much more.

Suppose, for example, that you are doing an assignment on the founders of the scientific field of sociology. Emile Durkheim would be one of those seminal sociological thinkers about whom you might want more information. Click on the SocioWeb entry and you will find a wealth of possibilities, including the one from the Durkheim Association, which will give you an opportunity to click on the following brief but highly useful biography of Durkheim.

Emile Durkheim (1858–1917)

David Emile Durkheim was born on April 15, 1858 in Epinal, capital town of the department of Vosges, in Lorraine. His mother, Mélanie, was a merchant's daughter, and his father, Moïse, had been rabbi of Epinal since the 1830s, and was also Chief Rabbi of the Vosges and Haute-Marne. Emile, whose grandfather and great-grandfather had also been rabbis, thus appeared destined for the rabbinate, and a part of his early education was spent in rabbinical school. This early ambition was dismissed while he was still a schoolboy, and soon after his arrival in Paris, Durkheim would break with Judaism altogether. But he always remained the product of close-knit, orthodox Jewish family, as well as that long-established Jewish community of Alsace-Lorraine that had been occupied by Prussian troops in 1870, and suffered the consequent anti-Semitism of the French citizenry. Later, Durkheim would argue that the hostility of Christianity toward Judaism had created an unusual sense of solidarity among the Jews.

An outstanding student at the Collège d'Epinal, Durkheim skipped two years, easily obtaining his baccalauréats in Letters (1874) and Sciences (1875), and distinguishing himself in the Concours Général. Intent now on becoming a teacher, Durkheim left Epinal for Paris to prepare for admission to the prestigious Ecole Normale Supérieure. Installed at a pension for non-resident students, however, he became utterly miserable: his father's illness left him anxious over his family's financial security; he was an utter provincial alone in Paris; and his intellectual predilections, already scientific rather than literary, were ill-fitted to the study of Latin and rhetoric essential for admission to the Ecole. After failing in his first two attempts at the entrance examination (in 1877 and 1878), Durkheim was at last admitted near the end of 1879.

Durkheim's generation at the Ecole was a particularly brilliant one, including not only the socialist Jean Jaurès, who became Durkheim's life-long friend, but also the philosophers Henri Bergson, Gustave Belot, Edmond Goblot, Felix Rauh, and Maurice Blondel, the psychologist Pierre Janet, the linguist Ferdinand Brunot, the historians Henri Berr and Camille Jullian, and the geographer Lucien Gallois. Despite constant fears of failure, which plagued him throughout his life, Durkheim became an active participant in the high-minded political and philosophical debates that characterized the Ecole; and, like Jaurès, he was soon a staunch advocate of the republican cause, with special admiration for Léon Gambetta, the brilliant orator and "spiritual embodiment" of the Third Republic, and the more moderate Jules Ferry, whose anti-clerical educational reforms would soon lead to a national system of free, compulsory, secular education.

Durkheim's concerns were less political than academic, however, and while he continued to criticise the literary rather than scientific emphasis of the Ecole, he discovered three scholars of a more congenial spirit—the philosophers Charles Renouvier and Emile Boutroux, and the historian Numas-Denis Fustel de Coulanges.

Though ill through much of 1881–82, Durkheim successfully passed his agrégation (the competitive examination required for admission to the teaching staff of state secondary schools, or lycées), and began teaching philosophy in 1882.

In 1882, the Faculty of Letters at Bordeaux had established France's first course in pedagogy for prospective school teachers, and in 1884 the state had begun to support it as part of its drive for a new system of secular, republican education. The course was first taught by Alfred Espinas, whose *Les Sociétés animales* (1877) Durkheim greatly admired, but who was soon elevated to Dean of the Faculty. Durkheim's articles on German philosophy and social science had by now caught the attention of Louis Liard, then Director of Higher Education in France. A devoted republican and Renouvierist, Liard both resented the German pre-eminence in social science and was intrigued by Durkheim's suggestions for the reconstruction of a secular, scientific French morality. At the instigation of Espinas and Liard, therefore, Durkheim was apponted in 1887 as "Chargé d'un Cours de Science Sociale et de Pédagogie" at Bordeaux. The "Science Sociale" was a concession to Durkheim, and it was under this guise that sociology now officially entered the French university system.

This appointment of a young social scientist to the predominantly humanist Faculty of Letters at Bordeaux was not without opposition, and Durkheim exacerbated this by emphasizing the value of sociology to the more traditional humanist disciplines of philosophy, history and law. He thus aroused (justifiable) fears of "sociological imperialism" and unjustifiable (though understandable) fears that his particular explanations of legal and moral institutions through reference to purely social causes undermined free will and individual moral agency. These fears long excluded Durkheim from the powerful Paris professorship to which he aspired. Nonetheless, he gained the support and even allegiance of at least some of his Bordeaux colleagues—the legal scholar Léon Duguit; the Roman historian Camille Jullian; the rationalist, neo-Kantian philosopher Octave Hamelin, and Georges Rodier, an expert on Aristotle. With Hamelin and Rodier, in particular, Durkheim formed a celebrated "trio" of rationalist opposition to those forms of mysticism and intuitionism which were increasingly denounced under the epithet "bergsonisme."

Throughout this Bordeaux period (1887–1902), Durkheim's primary responsibility was to lecture on the theory, history, and practice of education. Each Saturday morning, however, he also taught a public lecture course on social science, devoted to specialized studies of particular social phenomena, including social solidarity, family and kinship, incest, totemism, suicide, crime, religion, socialism, and law.

In 1898, Durkheim founded the *Année sociologique*, the first social science journal in France. In fact, Durkheim's intellectual virtuosity up to 1900 had implicitly contradicted one of his central arguments, namely that in modern societies, work (including intellectual work) should become more specialized, though remaining part of an organic whole. In 1896, therefore, putting aside his work on the history of socialism, Durkheim devoted himself to establishing a massive program of journalistic collaboration based upon a complex division of intellectual labor. Supported by a brilliant group of young scholars (mostly philosophers), the Année was to provide an annual survey of the strictly sociological literature, to provide additional information on studies in other specialized fields, and to publish original monographs in sociology.

As Director of Primary Education at the Ministry of Public Instruction from 1879 to 1896, Ferdinand Buisson had been the man most responsible for implementing Jules Ferry's educational reforms. Subsequently appointed to the chair in the Science of Education at the Sorbonne, Buisson was elected to the Chamber of Deputies in 1902, and the chair became vacant. The successful resolution of the Dreyfus Affair had left both sociology and socialism with a more respectable public image and Durkheim, while arguing that his competence in education was limited, and that his candidacy would thus give the appearance of using any expedient to insinuate himself in Paris, nonetheless allowed his name to go forward. After seeking letters from Boutroux, Buisson, and Victor Brochard, the Council of the Faculty of Letters at the Sorbonne appointed Durkheim chargé d'un course by a large majority. Four years later Durkheim was made professeur by a unanimous vote and assumed Buisson's chair, which was to be renamed "Science of Education and Sociology" in 1913.

Durkheim arrived in Paris with a reputation as a powerful intellect pursuing an aggressively scientific approach to all problems (everything else was mysticism, dilettantism, and irrationalism). His "science of morality" offended philosophers, his "science of religion" offended Catholics, and his appointment to the Sorbonne (which, in the wake of the Dreyfus Affair, appeared not above extra-academic considerations) offended those on the political Right. The appointment also gave Durkheim enormous power. His lecture courses were the only required courses at the Sorbonne, obligatory for all students seeking degrees in philosophy, history, literature, and languages; in addition, he was responsible for the education of successive generations of French school teachers, in whom he instilled all the fervour of his secular, rationalist morality. As an administrator, he sat on the Council of the University as well as on many other councils and committees throughout the University and the Ministry of Public Instruction, and though largely averse to politics, he numbered many powerful politicians among his personal friends. Not surprisingly, Durkheim's enemies complained of his power, accusing him of "managing" appointments and creating chairs of sociology in provincial universities in order to extend his influence. Frequently described as a "secular pope," Durkheim was viewed by critics as an agent of government anti-clericalism, and charged with seeking "a unique and pernicious domination over the minds of the young."

On August 3, 1914, Germany launched its invasion of Belgium and northern France. All went as in the summer of 1870 until the surprising Russians attacked East Prussia, forcing Moltke to withdraw troops for use on the eastern front. The French Army under Joffre regrouped with support from the British, and at the battle of the Marne, fought from September 5 to 12, forced the Germans to retreat, and thus altered the entire character of the war.

Durkheim's response was one of optimism and enthusiasm. Despite poor health already induced by overwork, he devoted himself to the cause of national defense, organizing a committee for the publication of studies and documents on the war, to be sent to neutral countries in the effort to undermine German propaganda. Several patriotic pamphlets were written by Durkheim himself, and sent to his fellow-countrymen in the effort to maintain the national pride. But for the most part, Durkheim was unaffected by the war hysteria, and, though always a patriot, was never a nationalist. Indeed, by 1916, he was concerned lest a German military defeat be turned to the advantage of the conservative, "clerical" party in France; and on at least two occasions, as a native of Alsace-Lorraine and as a Jew with a German name, Durkheim suffered aspersions of disloyalty motivated by the most vulgar kind of anti-Semitism.

The greatest blow, however, was yet to come. Durkheim was utterly devoted to his son André, a linguist who had gained his agrégation just before the War, and was among the most brilliant of the younger Année circle. Sent to the Bulgarian front late in 1915, André was declared missing in January, and in April, 1916, was confirmed dead.

Durkheim was devastated by his son's death, withdrawing into a "ferocious silence" and forbidding friends to even mention his son's name in his presence. Burying himself all the more in the war effort, he collapsed from a stroke after speaking passionately at one of his innumerable committee meetings. After resting for several months, relieved by America's entry into the war, he recovered sufficiently to again take up his work on La Morale; but on November 15, 1917, he died at the age of 59.

From Jones, R. A. 1986. Émile Durkheim. An Introduction to Four Major Works. Beverly Hills, London and New Delhi. For additional information, contact rajones@uxl.cso.uiuc.edu.

If you were interested in the basic methods of sociological research, you could click on the line included on the Collective Behavior page marked "Sociology Methods." This choice would lead you to many additional possibilities for material about the methods of sociological research. Similar choices are available for material about culture, social structure and organizations, and all the other subjects introduced in Parts 1 and 2 of *Sociology in a Changing World*.

Drawing the Data Down

For those who are interested in further explorations of census data, survey data, or case studies of this or any other changing society, the Internet offers unlimited resources. In *Sociology in a Changing World* and many other texts, census data are used to chart trends and changes in entire nations or in parts of them, particularly metropolitan regions. A good place to find data about populations is the U.S. Bureau of the Census (**www.census.gov**). To obtain a sociologically informed guide to population data on the Internet, including the relevant addresses, you should try the Population Council. Its Web address is **www.popcouncil.org.** Bring this up on your screen and you will find the quickest route to many population reference areas on the Internet. For example, one line will let you bring up a most useful Census Bureau Web page, shown here.

U.S. Census Bureau *the Official Statistics*
Topics in Text

● News ● Search
● Access Tools ● CenStats—CenStore
● Subjects A–Z ● Just for Fun
● About the Census ● User Manual ● New on the Site
● Pop Clock ● Economic Clock

Last Revised *Friday, 03-Jan-97 09:54:29*

This simple page offers entry into a wide variety of interactive pages where specific information and data are available. Suppose you are interested in immigration. Click on the box marked "Search" and you will receive a list of many subjects, each of which offers more information about a major area of population change, including one on immigration. That page (shown here) offers access to estimates and projections of immigrant populations in the United States, and more data about the foreign born in the United States and its states.

U.S. Census Bureau *the Official Statistics*
IMMIGRATION

The primary source for statistics on immigration is the **IMMIGRATION AND NATURALIZATION SERVICE** (INS). Their information office phone number is 202-305-1613

There are two sources of information about immigration on the Census Bureau's Internet site:

1. **Estimates and Projections**

   The U.S. Bureau of the Census uses immigration data from the INS and the decennial census, and other sources in our population estimates and projections programs. We modify the immigration data and combine it with other international movement data to display a component of population change labeled "net international migration." This component is comprised of:
   1. legal immigration from abroad,
   2. net undocumented immigration,
   3. emigration, and
   4. net movement between Puerto Rico and the U.S. mainland.

We have this component at the U.S., state, and county levels. You can locate this component in some of our estimates and projections offerings at:

2. The Current Population Survey

   The Current Population Survey provides data on the **Foreign Born** population for the nation and selected states. Foreign Born from this source includes:
   1. immigrants,
   2. refugees, and
   3. persons on temporary visas who are resident in the U.S. on the survey date.

Source: U.S. Census Bureau

Last Revised: Friday, 04-Oct-96 07:39:42
Please email comments (Please include your telephone number) to pop@census.gov.

Census Home   Subjects A–Z   Population Home

The page begins by noting that another treasure trove of data and information on immigration and related subjects is available from the U.S. Immigration and Naturalization Service. Note also that the original Census Bureau Web page offered the choice of a box marked "Access Tools." This will lead you to public domain software that you can download and use to access census data files that will permit you to do your own original research. This is the kind of research that is usually done in upper-level and graduate courses in demography, urban planning, economics, sociological methods, and criminology, but if you are interested in working with original data and are not reluctant to experiment with computer transfer of program and data files, this could lead you to a new realm of original sociological work.

If you are interested in working with other survey data, such as that used in your text, a good place to go is one of the various sociology departments that offer access to data. If you bring up the American Sociological Association web page (**www.asanet.org**) and go to the list of Sections, you will find another interactive entry for "Sociology Department Web Pages." This page lists many different sociology departments, some of which offer entry into excellent survey databases. Try Queens College. It offers access to the entire data set of the National Opinion Research Center General Social Survey. The sociologists at Queens College have also provided some excellent software that you can download. With this software and the data it will allow you to access, you can do some highly original research at any level of undergraduate or graduate sociology. The University of Michigan and the University of California at Berkeley also have Web pages on the American Sociological Association list that can lead you into survey data to download.

Exploring New Worlds of Research and Social Change

Any subject you care to mention can be researched on the Internet. You can also find out who is doing what to change the world. Just name your interest. Suppose you are interested in class, race, or gender, all of which are major topics at the heart of sociological theory and research. But these are also major areas of activity on the Internet, and not only among sociologists. For sociological guides through the mass of information on these subjects, you can follow leads offered by the various American Sociological Association Sections (including those devoted to class, race, and gender), or you can try a more general Sociological Server such as **www.webcom.com/dread/socio.html.** This page will offer you a great many leads into specific groups doing sociological research or engaging in social activism in an effort to address problems relating to race, class, and gender (among other major areas of social life).

The kinds of material available from official agencies and activist groups on the Internet may differ in important ways. This distinction should be kept in mind whenever you browse the Web for research or other purposes. The government agencies often give you official statistics and data on recent events; the social movement groups give you a more critical view of the official statistics and news releases. Suppose, for example, that you are interested in the AIDS epidemic. The U.S. Centers for Disease Control will offer a wider variety of analysis and data (**www.cdc.gov**) from an official point of view. This is helpful material, especially the latest domestic and international statistics about the spread of the disease or changes in treatment. For a more global perspective try the World Health Organization's Global Programme on AIDS (**http://gpawww.sho.ch/**). Again, this is an official agency of the United Nations and will offer a more governmental perspective on the data and recent events in treatment or AIDS policy. For the perspective of people involved in trying to influence official policy, try the Gay Men's Health Crisis Web page (**www.gmhc.org**). It will offer insight and criticism of official responses to the disease, along with opportunities to explore what other groups in the world of AIDS activism are saying and doing in the battle against the disease and against public indifference.

As you know, the subject of social inequality is a major area of sociology. Social-class differences seem to explain a great deal about the life chances of individuals and groups. And many changes are occurring in different social classes, especially the poor. Much attention is being given to the subject of homelessness, for example. A good source of information and data on homelessness in the United States and elsewhere is the National Coalition for the Homeless (**http://nch.ari.net/**). Here you will find a good deal of material on the connection between poverty and lack of shelter. You can also access pages about mental health and homelessness, drug and alcohol abuse issues, gender and racial issues in homelessness, advances and retreats in social policy, and much more.

A final example of a sociological world that you can explore on the Internet is that of criminology. The Internet offers a wider variety of resources on crime and the criminal justice system, starting with the FBI (**http://www.fbi.gov/**), where one can locate several sources of information about current and historical investigations. The FBI's home page offers links to monographs about the agency's most famous cases, including the capture of John Dillinger, investigations of Nazi saboteurs, and the Lindberg kidnapping. Press releases, hotlines on current unsolved crimes, congressional testimony, and downloadable files containing statistics from the *Uniform Crime Reports* are available.

The U.S. Department of Justice (**http://www.usdoj.gov/**) has a regularly updated home page with links to various agencies and projects. The Violence Against Women Office has a web site at **http://www.usdoj.gov/vawo/** with information on the National Domestic Violence Hotline. You will find the most recent federal legislation and regulations, research reports and case studies, and a Domestic Violence Awareness Manual targeted to federal employees but applicable to almost anyone. The Bureau of Justice Statistics, at **http://www.ojp.usdoj.gov/bjs/welcome.html,** provides statistics, most of which can be downloaded, about crimes and their victims, drugs and crime, and the criminal justice system. It also has links to other sources, such as the Federal Bureau of Prisons (**http://www.bop.gov/**), which provides statistics on the federal prison population, inmates and staff, broken down by age, ethnicity, race, sentences, types of offenses, and other variables. Research documents pertaining to the prison system are available, and most can be downloaded.

For an alternate view, try the innovative journal written for, by, and about inmates. The Journal of Prisoners on Prison (**http://www.synapse.net/~arrakis/jpp/jpp.html**) is published by prisoners whose purpose is "to bring the knowledge and experience of the incarcerated to bear upon more academic arguments and concerns and to inform public discourse about the current state of our carceral institutions." Here you can read material from people for whom imprisonment is or has been the reality of their daily existence. Articles have appeared on Native Americans in the prison system, prison education, attitude and behavior modification, the death penalty, and other topics.

In each of these areas of active sociological work we have mentioned just a few of the information resources available on the Internet. The point is to show you what kinds of material are available and to get you started in thinking about how to search for different types of material, from official statistics to the viewpoints of people directly involved in the social phenomena at issue.

A final suggestion: When you are browsing the Internet for a specific purpose, such as to find material for a research paper, try to discipline yourself to stay on course. It is very tempting to wander around the Web as various subjects strike your fancy. This can lead to interesting discoveries, but it can also burn up a lot of precious study time. Follow the leads that take you to the material you are looking for now. Save the addresses of other interesting Web pages for another occasion when you have more time. And good luck in all your searches.

Classic and Contemporary Readings

Part I: Social Foundation

OF THE DAWN OF FREEDOM
William E. B. DuBois

Throughout the world there is growing recognition of the pioneering role of William E. B. DuBois in establishing the discipline of sociology in the United States. DuBois's scholarly brilliance led him to become one of the very first African Americans to receive a Ph.D. at Harvard before the turn of the century. He earned his doctorate in philosophy because sociology was still viewed as a branch of that ancient field of social thought. Early in the twentieth century, American universities would begin to offer degrees in sociology as a discipline separate from philosophy, thanks in many respects to the seminal theoretical and empirical work carried out by DuBois.

The text highlights DuBois's original contributions to empirical research, which are especially evident in his social survey of Philadelphia's segregated black population late in the nineteenth century. The essay presented here reveals another side of DuBois's sociological imagination: his insights on the issues of freedom and racial identity for black Americans, as set forth in his famous book The Souls of Black Folk. *His discussion of the central place of African Americans in the making of the American nation, how their struggles to overcome the legacies of slavery have helped us understand the meaning of freedom, is world famous.*

DuBois was a sociologist who put his theories into practice. A social activist, he helped create America's foremost African American organizations, including the NAACP, and in so doing he demonstrated the ability of sociologists to serve both as scholars and as creators of positive social change.

The problem of the twentieth century is the problem of the color-line—the relation of the darker to the lighter races of men in Asia and Africa, in America and the islands of the sea. It was a phase of this problem that caused the Civil War; and however much they who marched South and North in 1861 may have fixed on the technical points of union and local autonomy as a shibboleth, all nevertheless knew, as we know, that the question of Negro slavery was the real cause of the conflict. Curious it was, too, how this deeper question ever forced itself to the surface despite effort and disclaimer. No sooner had Northern armies touched Southern soil than this old question, newly guised, sprang from the earth—What shall be done with Negroes? Peremptory military commands, this way and that, could not answer the query; the Emancipation Proclamation seemed but to broaden and intensify the difficulties; and the War Amendments made the Negro problems of today.

It is the aim of this essay to study the period of history from 1861 to 1872 so far as it relates to the American Negro. In effect, this tale of the dawn of Freedom is an account of that government of men called the Freedmen's Bureau—one of the most singular and interesting of the attempts made by a great nation to grapple with vast problems of race and social condition. . . .

It was a Pierce of Boston who pointed out the way, and thus became in a sense the founder of the Freedmen's Bureau. He was a firm friend of Secretary Chase; and when, in 1861, the care of slaves and abandoned lands developed upon the Treasury officials, Pierce was specially detailed from the ranks to study the conditions. First, he cared for the refugees at Fortress Monroe; and then, after Sherman had captured Hilton Head, Pierce was sent there to found his Port Royal experiment of making free workingmen out of slaves. Before his experiment was barely started, however, the problem of the fugitives had assumed such proportions that it was taken from the hands of the over-burdened Treasury Department and given to the army officials. Already centres of massed freedmen were forming at Fortress Monroe, Washington, New Orleans, Vicksburg and Corinth, Columbus, Ky., and Cairo, Ill., as well as at Port Royal. Army chaplains found here new and fruitful fields; "superintendents of contrabands" multiplied, and some attempt at systematic work was made by enlisting the able-bodied men and giving work to the others.

Then came the Freedmen's Aid societies, born of the touching appeals from Pierce and from these other centres of distress. There was the American Missionary Association, sprung from the *Amistad,* and now full-grown for work; the various church organizations, the National Freedmen's Relief Association, the American Freedmen's Union, the Western Freedmen's Aid Commission—in all fifty or more active organizations, which sent clothes, money, school-books, and teachers southward. All they did was needed, for the destitution of the freedmen was often reported as "too appalling for belief," and the situation was daily growing worse rather than better.

And daily, too, it seemed more plain that this was no ordinary matter of temporary relief, but a national crisis; for here loomed a labor problem of vast dimensions. Masses of Negroes stood idle, or, if they worked spasmodically, were never sure of pay; and if perchance they received pay, squandered the new thing thoughtlessly. In these and other ways were camp-life and the new liberty demoralizing the freedmen. The broader economic organization thus clearly demanded sprang up here and there as accident and local conditions determined. Here it was that Pierce's Port Royal plan of leased plantations and guided workmen pointed out the rough way. In Washington the military governor, at the urgent appeal of the superintendent, opened confiscated estates to the cultivation of the fugitives, and there in the shadow of the dome gathered black farm villages. General Dix gave over estates to the freedmen of Fortress Monroe, and so on, South and West. The government and benevolent societies furnished the means of cultivation, and the Negro turned again slowly to work. The systems of control, thus started, rapidly grew, here and there, into strange little governments, like that of General Banks in Louisiana, with its ninety thousand black subjects, its fifty thousand guided laborers, and its annual budget of one hundred thousand dollars and more. It made out four thousand pay-rolls a year, registered all freedmen, inquired into grievances and redressed them, laid and collected taxes, and established a system of public schools. So, too, Colonel Eaton, the superintendent of Tennessee and Arkansas, ruled over one hundred thousand freedmen, leased and cultivated seven thousand acres of cotton land, and fed ten thousand paupers a year. In South Carolina was General Saxton, with his deep interest in black folk. He succeeded Pierce and the Treasury officials, and sold forfeited estates, leased abandoned plantations, encouraged schools, and received from Sherman, after that terribly picturesque march to the sea, thousands of wretched camp followers.

Three characteristic things one might have seen in Sherman's raid through Georgia, which threw the new situation in shadowy relief; the Conqueror, the Conquered, and the Negro. Some see all significance in the grim front of the destroyer, and some in the bitter sufferers of the Lost Cause. But to me neither soldier nor fugitive speaks with so deep a meaning as that dark human cloud that hung like remorse on the rear of those swift columns, swelling at times to half their size, almost engulfing and choking them. In vain were they ordered back, in vain were bridges hewn from beneath their feet; on they trudged and writhed and surged, until they rolled into Savannah, a starved and naked horde of tens of thousands. There too came the characteristic military remedy: "The islands from Charleston south, the abandoned rice-fields along the rivers for thirty miles back from the sea, and the country bordering the St. John's River, Florida, and reserved and set apart for the settlement of Negroes now made free by act of war." So read the celebrated "Field-order Number Fifteen.

All these experiments, orders, and systems were bound to attract and perplex the government and the nation. Directly after the Emancipation Proclamation, Representative Eliot had introduced a bill creating a Bureau of Emancipation; but it was never reported. The following June a committee of inquiry, appointed by the Secretary of War, reported in favor of a temporary bureau for the "improvement, protection, and employment of refugee freedmen," on much the same lines as were afterwards followed. Petitions came in to President Lincoln from distinguished citizens and organizations, strongly urging a comprehensive and unified plan of dealing with the freedmen, under a bureau which should be "charged with the study of plans and execution of measures for easily guiding, and in every way judiciously and humanely aiding, the passage of our emancipated and yet to be emancipated blacks from the old condition of forced labor to their new state of voluntary industry."

Some half-hearted steps were taken to accomplish this, in part, by putting the whole matter again in charge of the special Treasury agents. Laws of 1863 and 1864 directed them to take charge of and lease abandoned lands for periods not exceeding twelve months, and to "provide in such leases, or otherwise, for the employment and general welfare" of the freedmen. Most of the army officers greeted this as a welcome relief from perplexing "Negro affairs," and Secretary Fessenden, July 29, 1864, issued an excellent system of regulations, which were afterward closely followed by General Howard. Under Treasury agents, large quantities of land were leased in the Mississippi Valley, and many Negroes were employed; but in August, 1864, the new regulations were suspended for reasons of "public policy," and the army was again in control.

Meanwhile Congress had turned its attention to the subject; and in March the House passed a bill by a majority of two establishing a Bureau for Freedmen in the War Department. Charles Sumner, who had charge of the bill in the Senate, argued that freedmen and abandoned lands ought to be under the same department, and reported a substitute for the House bill attaching the Bureau to the Treasury Department. This bill passed, but too late for action by the House. The debates wandered over the whole policy of the administration and the general question of slavery, without touching very closely the specific merits of the measure in hand. Then the national election took place; and the administration, with a vote of renewed confidence from the country, addressed itself to the matter more seriously. A conference between the two branches of Congress agreed upon a carefully drawn measure which contained the chief provisions of Sumner's bill, but made the proposed organization a department independent of both the War and the Treasury officials. The bill was conservative, giving the new department "general superintendence of all freedmen." Its purpose was to "establish regulations" for them, protect them, lease them lands, adjust their wages, and appear in civil and military courts as their "next friend." There were many limitations attached to the powers thus granted, and the organization was made permanent. Nevertheless, the Senate defeated the bill, and a new conference committee was appointed. This committee reported a new bill, February 28, which was whirled through just as the session closed, and became the act of 1865 establishing in the War Department a "Bureau of Refugees, Freedmen, and Abandoned Lands."

This last compromise was a hasty bit of legislation, vague and uncertain in outline. A Bureau was created, "to continue during the present war of Rebellion, and for one year thereafter," to which was given "the supervision and management of all abandoned lands and the control of all subjects relating to refugees and freedmen," under "such rules and regulations as may be presented by the head of the Bureau and approved by the President." A Commissioner, appointed by the President and Senate, was to control the Bureau, with an office force not exceeding ten clerks. The President might also appoint assistant commissioners in the seceded States, and to all these offices military officials might be detailed at regular pay. The Secretary of War could issue rations, clothing, and fuel to the destitute, and all abandoned property was placed in the hands of the Bureau for eventual lease and sale to ex-slaves in forty-acre parcels.

Thus did the United States government definitely assume charge of the emancipated Negro as the ward of the nation. It was a tremendous undertaking. Here at a stroke of the pen was erected a government of millions of men—and not ordinary men either, but black men emasculated by a peculiarly complete system of slavery, centuries old; and now, suddenly, violently, they come into a new birthright, at a time of war and passion, in the midst of the stricken and embittered population of their former masters. Any man might well have hesitated to assume charge of such a work, with vast responsibilities, indefinite powers, and limited resources. Probably no one but a soldier would have answered such a call promptly; and, indeed, no one but a soldier could be called, for Congress had appropriated no money for salaries and expenses.

Less than a month after the weary Emancipator passed to his rest, his successor assigned Major-Gen. Oliver O. Howard to duty as Commissioner of the new Bureau. He was a Maine man, then only thirty-five years of age. He had marched with Sherman to the sea, had fought well at Gettysburg, and but the year before had been assigned to the command of the Department of Tennessee. An honest man, with too much faith in human nature, little aptitude for business and intricate detail, he had had large opportunity of becoming acquainted at first hand with much of the work before him. And of that work it has been truly said that "no approximately correct history of civilization can ever be written which does not throw out in bold relief, as one of the great landmarks of political and social progress, the organization and administration of the Freedmen's Bureau."

On May 12, 1865, Howard was appointed; and he assumed the duties of his office promptly on the 15th, and began examining the field of work. A curious mess he looked upon: little despotisms, communistic experiments, slavery, peonage, business speculations, organized charity, unorganized almsgiving—all reeling on under the guise of helping the freedmen, and all enshrined in the smoke and blood of war and the cursing and silence of angry men. On May 19 the new government—for a government it really was—issued its constitution; commissioners were to be appointed in each of the seceded states, who were to take charge of "all subjects relating to refugees and freedmen," and all relief and rations were to be given by their consent alone. The Bureau invited continued coöperation with benevolent societies, and declared: "It will be the object of all commissioners to introduce practicable systems of compensated labor," and to establish schools. Forthwith nine assistant commissioners were appointed. They were to hasten to their fields of work; seek gradually to close relief establishments, and make the destitute self-supporting; act as courts of law where there were no courts, or where Negroes were not recognized in them as free; establish the institution of marriage among ex-slaves, and keep records; see that freedmen were free to choose their employers, and help in making fair contracts for them; and finally, the circular said: "Simple good faith, for which we hope on all hands for those concerned in the passing away of slavery, will especially relieve the assistant commissioners in the discharge of their duties toward the freedmen, as well as promote the general welfare."

No sooner was the work thus started, and the general system and local organization in some measure begun, than two grave difficulties appeared which changed largely the theory and outcome of Bureau work. First, there were the abandoned lands of the South. It had long been the more or less definitely expressed theory of the North that all the chief problems of Emancipation might be settled by establishing the slaves on the forfeited lands of their masters—a sort of poetic justice, said some. But this poetry done into solemn prose meant either wholesale confiscation of private property in the South, or vast appropriations. Now Congress had not appropriated a cent, and no sooner did the proclamations of general amnesty appear than the eight hundred thousand acres of abandoned lands in the hands of the Freedmen's Bureau melted quickly away. The second difficulty lay in perfecting the local organization of the Bureau throughout the wide field of work. Making a new machine and sending out officials of duly ascertained fitness for a great work of social reform is no child's task; but this task was even harder, for a new central organization had to be fitted on a heterogeneous and confused but already existing system of relief and control of ex-slaves; and the agents available for this work must be sought for in an army still busy with war operations—men in the very nature of the case ill fitted for delicate social work—or among the questionable camp followers of an invading host. Thus, after a year's work, vigorously as it was pushed, the problem looked even more difficult to grasp and solve than at the beginning. Nevertheless, three things that year's work did, well worth the doing: it relieved a vast amount of physical suffering; it transported seven thousand fugitives from congested centres back to the farm; and, best of all, it inaugurated the crusade of the New England schoolma'am.

The annals of this Ninth Crusade are yet to be written—the tale of a mission that seemed to our age far more quixotic than the quest of St. Louis seemed to his. Behind the mists of ruin and rapine waved the calico dresses of women who dared, and after the hoarse mouthings of the field guns rang the rhythm of the alphabet. Rich and poor they were, serious and curious. Bereaved now of a father, now of a brother, now of more than these, they came seeking a life work in planting New England schoolhouses among the white and black of the South. They did their work well. In that first year they taught one hundred thousand souls, and more.

Evidently, Congress must soon legislate again on the hastily organized Bureau, which had so quickly grown into wide significance and vast possibilities. An institution such as that was well-nigh as difficult to end as to begin. Early in 1866 Congress took up the matter, when Senator Trumbull, of Illinois, introduced a bill to extend the Bureau and enlarge its powers. This measure received, at the hands of Congress, far more thorough discussion and attention than its predecessor. The war cloud had thinned enough to allow a clearer conception of the work of Emancipation. The champions of the bill argued that the strengthening of the Freedmen's Bureau was still a military necessity; that it was needed for the proper carrying out of the Thirteenth Amendment, and was a work of sheer justice to the ex-slave, at a trifling cost to the government. The opponents of the measure declared that the war was over, and the necessity for war measures past; that the Bureau, by reason of its extraordinary powers, was clearly unconstitutional in time of peace, and was destined to irritate the South and pauperize the freedmen, at a final cost of possibly hundreds of millions. These two arguments were unanswered, and indeed unanswerable: the one that the extraordinary powers of the Bureau threatened the civil rights of all citizens; and the other that the government must have power to do what manifestly must be done, and that present abandonment of the freedmen meant their practical re-enslavement. The bill which finally passed enlarged and made permanent the Freedmen's Bureau. It was promptly vetoed by President Johnson as "unconstitutional," "unnecessary," and "extrajudicial," and failed of passage over the veto. Meantime, however, the breach between Congress and the President began to broaden, and a modified form of the lost bill was finally passed over the President's second veto, July 16.

The act of 1866 gave the Freedmen's Bureau its final form—the form by which it will be known to posterity and judged of men. It extended the existence of the Bureau to July, 1868; it authorized additional assistant commissioners, the retention of army officers mustered out of regular service, the sale of certain forfeited lands to freedmen on nominal terms, the sale of Confederate public property for Negro schools, and a wider field of judicial interpretation and cognizance. The government of the unreconstructed South was thus put very largely in the hands of the Freedmen's Bureau, especially as in many cases the departmental military commander was now made also assistant commissioner. It was thus that the Freedmen's Bureau became a full-fledged government of men. It made laws, executed them and interpreted them; it laid and collected taxes, defined and punished crime, maintained and used military force, and dictated such measures as it thought necessary and proper for the accomplishment of its varied ends. Naturally, all these powers were not exercised continuously nor to their fullest extent; and yet, as General Howard has said, "scarcely any subject that has to be legislated upon in civil society failed, at one time or another, to demand the action of this singular Bureau. . . ."

It is doubly difficult to write of this period calmly, so intense was the feeling, so mighty the human passions that swayed and blinded men. Amid it all, two figures ever stand to typify that day to coming ages—the one, a gray-haired gentleman, whose fathers had quit themselves like men, whose sons lay in nameless graves; who bowed to the evil of slavery because its abolition threatened untold ill to all; who stood at last, in the evening of life, a blighted, ruined form, with hate in his eyes—and the other, a form hovering dark and mother-like; her awful face black with the mists of centuries, had aforetime quailed at that white master's command, had bent in love over the cradles of his sons and daughters, and closed in death the sunken eyes of his wife—aye, too, at his behest had laid herself low to his lust, and borne a tawny man-child to the world, only to see her dark boy's limbs scattered to the winds by midnight marauders riding after "damned Niggers." These were the saddest sights of that woeful day; and no man clasped the hands of these two passing figures of the present-past; but, hating, they went to their long home, and, hating, their children's children live to-day.

Here, then, was the field of work for the Freedmen's Bureau; and since, with some hesitation, it was continued by the act of 1868 until 1869, let us look upon four years of its work as a whole. There were, in 1868, nine hundred Bureau officials scattered from Washington to Texas, ruling, directly and indirectly, many millions of men. The deeds of these rulers fall mainly under seven heads: the relief of physical suffering, the overseeing of the beginnings of free labor, the buying and selling of land, the establishment of schools, the paying of bounties, the administration of justice, and the financiering of all these activities.

Up to June, 1869, over half a million patients had been treated by Bureau physicians and surgeons, and sixty hospitals and asylums had been in operation. In fifty months twenty-one million free rations were distributed at a cost of over four million dollars. Next came the difficult question of labor. First, thirty thousand black men were transported from the refuges and relief stations back to the farms, back to the critical trial of a new way of working. Plain instructions went out from Washington: the laborers must be free to choose their employers, no fixed rate of wages was prescribed, and there was to be no peonage or forced labor. So far, so good; but where local agents differed *toto cœlo* in capacity and character, where the *personnel* was continually changing, the outcome was necessarily varied. The largest element of success lay in the fact that the majority of the freedmen were willing, even eager, to work. So labor contracts were written—fifty thousand in a single State—laborers advised, wages guaranteed, and employers supplied. In truth, the organization became a vast labor bureau—not perfect, indeed, notably defective here and there, but on the whole successful beyond the dreams of thoughtful men. The two great obstacles which confronted the officials were the tyrant and the idler—the slaveholder who was determined to perpetuate slavery under another name; and the freedman who regarded freedom as perpetual rest—the Devil and the Deep Sea.

In the work of establishing the Negroes as peasant proprietors, the Bureau was from the first handicapped and at last absolutely checked. Something was done, and larger things were planned; abandoned lands were leased so long as they remained in the hands of the Bureau, and a total revenue of nearly half a million dollars derived from black tenants. Some other lands to which the nation had gained title were sold on easy terms, and public lands were opened for settlement to the very few freedmen who had tools and capital. But the vision of "forty acres and a mule"—the righteous and reasonable ambition to become a landholder, which the nation had all but categorically promised the freedmen—was destined in most cases to bitter disappointment. And those men of marvellous hindsight who are today seeking to preach the Negro back to the present peonage of the soil know well, or ought to know, that the opportunity of binding the Negro peasant willingly to the soil was lost on that day when the Commissioner of the Freedmen's Bureau had to go to South Carolina and tell the weeping freedmen, after their years of toil, that their land was not theirs, that there was a mistake—somewhere. If by 1874 the Georgia Negro alone owned three hundred and fifty thousand acres of land, it was by grace of his thrift rather than by bounty of the government.

The greatest success of the Freedmen's Bureau lay in the planting of the free school among Negroes, and the idea of free elementary education among all classes in the South. It not only called the school-mistresses through the benevolent agencies and built them school-houses, but it helped discover and support such apostles of human culture as Edmund Ware, Samuel Armstrong and Erastus Cravath. The opposition to Negro education in the South was at first bitter, and showed itself in ashes, insult, and blood; for the South believed an educated Negro to be a dangerous Negro. And the South was not wholly wrong; for education among all kinds of men always has had, and always will have, an element of danger and revolution, of dissatisfaction and discontent. Nevertheless, men strive to know. Perhaps some inkling of this paradox, even in the unquiet days of the Bureau, helped the bayonets allay an opposition to human training which still to-day lies smouldering in the South, but not flaming. Fisk, Atlanta, Howard, and Hampton were founded in these days, and six million dollars were expended for educational work, seven hundred and fifty thousand dollars of which the freedmen themselves gave of their poverty.

Such contributions, together with the buying of land and various other enterprises, showed that the ex-slave was handling some free capital already. The chief initial source of this was labor in the army, and his pay and bounty as a soldier. Payments to Negro soldiers were at first complicated by the ignorance of the recipients, and the fact that the quotas of colored regiments from Northern States were largely filled by recruits from the South, unknown to their fellow soldiers. Consequently, payments were accompanied by such frauds that Congress, by joint resolution in 1867, put the whole matter in the hands of the Freedmen's Bureau. In two years six million dollars was thus distributed to five thousand claimants, and in the end the sum exceeded eight million dollars. Even in this system fraud was frequent; but still the work put needed capital in the hands of practical paupers, and some, at least, was well spent.

The most perplexing and least successful part of the Bureau's work lay in the exercise of its judicial functions. The regular Bureau court consisted of one representative of the employer, one of the Negro, and one of the Bureau. If the Bureau could have maintained a perfectly judicial attitude, this arrangement would have been ideal, and must in time have gained confidence; but the nature of its other activities and the character of its *personnel* prejudiced the Bureau in favor of the black litigants, and led without doubt to much injustice and annoyance. On the other hand, to leave the Negro in the hands of Southern courts was impossible. In a distracted land where slavery had hardly fallen, to keep the strong from wanton abuse of the weak, and the weak from gloating insolently over the half-shorn strength of the strong, was a thankless, hopeless task. The former masters of the land were peremptorily ordered about, seized, and imprisoned, and punished over and again, with scant courtesy from army officers. The former slaves were intimidated, beaten, raped, and butchered by angry and revengeful men. Bureau courts tended to become centres simply for punishing whites, while the regular civil courts tended to become solely institutions for perpetuating the slavery of blacks. Almost every law and method ingenuity could devise was employed by the legislatures to reduce the Negroes to serfdom—to make them the slaves of the State, if not of individual owners; while the Bureau officials too often were found striving to put the "bottom rail on top," and gave the freedmen a power and independence which they could not yet use. It is all well enough for us of another generation to wax wise with advice to those who bore the burden in the heat of the day. It is full easy now to see that the man who lost home, fortune, and family at a stroke, and saw his land ruled by "mules and niggers," was really benefited by the passing of slavery. It is not difficult now to say to the young freedman, cheated and cuffed about who has seen his father's head beaten to a jelly and his own mother namelessly assaulted, that the meek shall inherit the earth. Above all, nothing is more convenient than to heap on the Freedmen's Bureau all the evils of that evil day, and damn it utterly for every mistake and blunder that was made.

All this is easy, but it is neither sensible nor just. Some one had blundered, but that was long before Oliver Howard was born; there was criminal aggression and heedless neglect, but without some system of control there would have been far more than there was. Had that control been from within, the Negro would have been re-enslaved, to all intents and purposes. Coming as the control did from without, perfect men and methods would have bettered all things; and even with imperfect agents and questionable methods, the work accomplished was not undeserving of commendation.

Such was the dawn of Freedom; such was the work of the Freedmen's Bureau, which, summed up in brief, may be epitomized thus: for some fifteen million dollars, beside the sums spent before 1865, and the dole of benevolent societies, this Bureau set going a system of free labor, established a beginning of peasant proprietorship, secured the recognition of black freedmen before courts of law, and founded the free common school in the South. On the other hand, it failed to begin the establishment of good-will between ex-masters and freedmen, to guard its work wholly from paternalistic methods which discouraged self-reliance, and to carry out to any considerable extent its implied promises to furnish the freedmen with land. Its successes were the result of hard work, supplemented by the aid of philanthropists and the eager striving of black men. Its failures were the result of bad local agents, the inherent difficulties of the work, and national neglect.

QUESTIONS

1. When we say that William E. B. DuBois was one of the first empirical sociologists, what kind of sociological work are we referring to? Give an example of his empirical research from the text.

2. Explain in your own terms the statement at the beginning of the essay that "[t]he problem of the twentieth century is the problem of the color-line—the relation of the darker to the lighter races of men in Asia and Africa, in America and the islands of the sea." Give recent examples from the United States that would support this statement.

PROSTITUTION, DRUG USE, AND AIDS

Claire Sterk

This article describes how sociologists work to become accepted among people whom they wish to understand and write about. The author, Claire Sterk, conducted an extensive study of drug users and prostitutes in three cities on the East Coast, applying the research method known as ethnography or "field research." In ethnographic research the sociologist attempts to accurately describe a great many aspects of a community or group. This means that he or she must understand their culture, their social structure, and how these are changing as a result of social forces occurring either within or outside the specific community or group.

Field research also requires that the researcher know how the people being observed understand their social world and how they explain their actions to themselves. This means that the researcher must spend a great deal of time getting to know those people on a very human and often intimate basis. But if we are to know people well enough so that they will feel comfortable sharing their feelings and problems with us, they must trust us. They must not feel that we are there to exploit them or to pry into their private lives. Most people welcome opportunities to tell the stories of their lives to others, but they also want to feel that the person in whom they are confiding understands them. Yet if we are too understanding and compassionate we may lose our ability to sort out fact from fiction. Thus, of all the sociological methods, ethnographic field research requires the greatest sensitivity to human feelings and interaction.

In her field research, Sterk was especially interested in discovering whether and to what extent women who become involved in prostitution through cocaine and crack use are at risk of contracting AIDS. Although she was an outsider to those she was observing, her presence was accepted by them because she was "out there"—in motels and hotels, brothels and escort services, shooting galleries and crack houses. In this selection she describes some of her experiences in the field and her feelings about them.

During the summer of 1986 I began conducting research among drug users and prostitutes in the New York metropolitan area. I had studied comparable groups in the Netherlands and was interested in discovering similarities and differences between the ways of life of these populations on both sides of the Atlantic Ocean. One can argue that turning tricks and shooting dope are the same all over the world. In reality, however, there are differences created by varying cultural circumstances. For example, in New York, where prostitution is illegal, the pimp plays a more important role in the prostitute's life than is the case in the Netherlands. When it comes to drugs, significant differences accrue from the fact that Dutch policies regarding drugs are more liberal than U.S. policies; moreover, crack has not yet become popular in the Netherlands.

Most of my research was done in Manhattan and Brooklyn and in northeastern New Jersey. Prostitutes and drug users frequently travel between New York and New Jersey. The two regions are close enough together so that the time it takes to travel between them amounts to less than thirty minutes. Operating in two adjacent states has advantages if one is involved in illegal activities; for one thing, it enables one to avoid an arrest warrant. If the police are seeking prostitutes in New York, the women simply shift their operation across the state line. Those living in New Jersey also cite economic reasons for commuting: In a large city like New York it is easier to make money, while the costs of living are significantly lower in New Jersey.

Before undertaking ethnographic research among people who are involved in deviant and very often illegal activities, one must locate the target population and determine how best to approach potential informants. With the help of colleagues, taxi drivers, and others, I was able to identify prostitute "strolls" and drug copping areas. I began visiting these neighborhoods and tried to get a sense of key events and characters by hanging out there. This gave me a chance to familiarize myself with the area while at the same time enabling the "regulars" to get to know my "face." Knowing where to go and recognizing faces, however, is only the beginning of a research effort. One can learn only so much through observation. The researcher must interact with the people he or she is studying.

A researcher—a stranger—cannot simply walk up to a potential informant and start chatting with him or her, especially if the informant is involved in illegal activities. When initiating a conversation, the researcher must justify his or her presence and indicate the desire for interaction, usually without knowing whether the other person can be trusted. Gaining trust is very important.

My acceptance into the prostitute subculture came about in a rather unexpected way. I had been walking around on the stroll for days and nobody wanted to talk to me. I recognized a few of the prostitutes from earlier visits, but they ignored me. But finally one of them, Ann, responded to my greeting. In a very cynical tone she asked me if I was looking for something special. For a second I did not know what to say. I answered very vaguely that I was just walking around. She thought this to be a silly answer and asked aggressively where I was from. I told her Amsterdam and started talking more openly. She teased me because I was getting red in the face. I kept on talking, glad that I had finally caught somebody's attention. I told her I was interested in prostitution and wanted to find out about the situation in the United States.

Ann challenged my knowledge, and apparently I answered her questions appropriately. She started talking about one of her girlfriends who was in "the life" and had moved to Europe with a boyfriend, an American GI stationed in West Germany. After the relationship ended, she began working in the sex business in Amsterdam. I was familiar with the club Ann mentioned and knew its owner. Ann began to open up and talk more to me, but she was careful. Another prostitute came by to check out what we were doing. Ann became very defensive about her relationship with me. She told the other woman to knock off, and described me as one of her friends.

I was fortunate, not only because Ann was willing to talk with me but also because I was not completely naive. Being somewhat familiar with the life style of the persons studied is of great value to a researcher in the field. The researcher will never have the knowledge of an insider without becoming a member of the group being studied, but a good ethnographer will try to find out about the norms and values of the world he or she is studying—always keeping in mind that too much knowledge might be seen as threatening.

In another situation I gained the confidence of an informant named Mo by demonstrating my knowledge of three-card monte, a popular con game. A white woman from Europe is not supposed to have such knowledge. My "showing off" made Goldman, a pimp, curious. Goldman, who has a penchant for big cars and lots of jewelry, said to me, "Damn, baby, you know what you are talking about. That's good, though; otherwise they would try to fool you. You have to prove yourself; showing off is what matters. Don't show off too much, now. We don't need wiseguys around here. I will tell you what to do and I will give my ladies instructions. If you are nice we won't have any problems."

While talking with potential informants, the researcher also develops a sense of who the important "players" are. It is necessary to gain their trust. They provide an entree into the community under study by facilitating the process of gaining the trust of others. Ideally, key contacts are individuals who are known and respected by other members of the community. Ann, for example, was one of the "main ladies"; Mo, a three-card monte player, was viewed as a good hustler; and Goldman was a well-known pimp.

During the initial stages of my research I was not the only one exploring and wondering. Respondents often tried to place me in impossible positions. Rumors spread that I was a potential prostitute, a drug user, or an undercover police officer. I was friendly, and so were my respondents, but simultaneously they were contemplating the possibility that I had a "hidden agenda." Mistrust and suspicion were ever-present, even in contacts with key respondents. Ann, for example, would, when I least expected it, ask me to repeat a certain story I had told her. She also explained to me that in trusting me she was taking chances herself. She would be blamed if it turned out that I could not be trusted, and this would have negative repercussions for her reputation.

One of the main lessons I have learned is that I must be honest and open about my intentions and that I must be constantly alert to the feelings of respondents. Being trusted does not assure acceptance. Again and again people challenged my presence and tested my intentions to "see if I was for real." Street life seems to require that one never develop permanent trust for anyone. One must continually check and reassess.

On one occasion I was standing on the street where the prostitutes were usually picked up by their customers. It was a nice evening, but business was slow. Pat, one of the streetwalkers, started telling me how they had been observing me. "We did not know if you were for real," she said. "It looked like we could trust you, but that could be your game. We decided to leave you alone and see how you would handle the tricks. I never forget the time the guy kept waving at you and you just looked around to see what we were doing. You couldn't have done better. He is still one of my regulars."

Pat and I now can laugh together about that situation. I referred the customer to her, telling him I was just hanging out on my night off.

There were many other episodes in which people tested my integrity, either by observing my reactions or by asking me for favors. The prostitutes would ask me to hold their purses, or they would share stories and check later to see if I had gossiped. They expected me to buy them a cup of coffee or a sandwich and to drive them around as if I were a cab driver. Ann advised me: "You have to be nice, but don't act like a softie!" I was also (unknowingly) used as "bait" for customers. Our tacit agreement was that I would not alienate the men who stopped to talk to me; instead, I would direct them to the "working girls."

Setting limits was a major issue. Repeatedly I had to convince drug users that I had no interest in buying stolen goods, and I often had to demonstrate to pimps that I was not interested in working for them. I was involved in the groups I was studying, but I remained an outsider in many ways. I was an outsider not only because I was not an active participant or because of my Dutch accent, but also because frequently I was one of the few, if not the only, white person in the area. This made me highly visible and easy to recognize. I was teasingly referred to as "the white girl," "Whitie," or "Miss Whitie," and one of the pimps told me he had a special deal for white ladies. The teasing had a bonding effect; several women expressed this by saying, "You are my only white friend" or "You are a nice white person."

During the many hours I spent with the prostitutes, of whom many were drug users, their pimps, drug partners, and dealers seldom interrupted their illegal activities because of my presence. Occasionally I was asked to leave the area because my presence was seen as a problem. The drug-using activities were generally covert and usually took place indoors, whereas the prostitution deals were more public.

Most of the women would talk with me about their work if I asked them about it, although they seldom discussed their work among themselves. (An exception was talk about tricks who could not be trusted or were too demanding.) Frequently they told me stories, mainly dealing with their emotions, that they did not share with one another. In short, I was treated as a trusted outsider who had a sense of what was going on in their lives.

My outsider status was validated on the occasions when I was seen as incompetent on the street. For example, everybody enjoyed my initial inability to anticipate police presence. I would be stopped and told to leave; my hidden audience would later make fun of me, but at the same time ensure that I didn't get into trouble. They also informed me about the dangers involved in being out on the street. "Prostitutes are not staying out late anymore," I was told. "A group of four young men have been coming into the area. They wait until it gets dark and start assaulting the women. The moment one of the women is alone, they jump on her, take her money, and hurt her."

The women became even more frightened after one of them was killed. Paula said to me, "You should not come here after dark. We are from the street . . . I am not saying that I am stronger than you are, but you do not have to be out here. I won't come unless I have to. I am even storing dope so I don't have to go out late at night."

It was during these moments that I realized that I would always be an outsider. No matter how much time I spent with them, I could always return to another world, a world of safety and stability. I often felt bad about this, and about the fact that there was nothing I could do to change their situation. These feelings became stronger the more I was confronted with the consequences of the AIDS epidemic.

By now it is widely known that many groups besides homosexual males are at risk of contracting AIDS. Among those groups are intravenous drug users, sexually active individuals and their sexual partners, and their babies. In the New York metropolitan area infection rates among intravenous drug users are as high as they are among homosexual men. During the hours I spent talking with respondents, I tried to sensitize them to the risks they were taking, and we talked about the possibility of modifying their behavior. Condom use and needle sharing were frequent topics of discussion.

One evening I was sitting with three of the prostitutes. An outreach worker had visited the stroll and they had plenty of condoms. We were joking, but at the same time we were talking about safe sex. The women's opinions about condom use varied. Laura said she never used them. Cindy would not have sex without a condom, and Maria used condoms with her tricks but not with her boyfriend. Maria's boyfriend gets upset if she so much as shows him a condom. All three agreed that it is easier to propose the use of condoms with tricks than with steadies. But as Laura pointed out, "I'm not going to fight about it. What's the big deal? He'll turn around and find somebody else, if that's what he wants. I always check to see if they are clean anyhow."

Our conversation shifted to blow jobs. Their mood was playful but serious. Cindy told me to taste a rubber before I made any further comments. She has learned how to use a condom while having oral sex without the customer knowing it. She is very proud of this skill and provided a demonstration. Giggling, we tried to follow her instructions. I do not know if this made a lasting impression on Laura and Maria, but at least we brought the issue out into the open.

On another occasion one of the prostitutes, Angie, said that she didn't think using condoms made any difference. "I'm already in the gutter," she said. "I feel sick, am losing weight. I'm going to die anyhow. What fucking difference does it make?"

We talked about knowledge, attitudes, and behaviors, and about the relevance of testing for HIV antibodies. Sometimes I initiated these discussions; at other times I was drawn into an ongoing conversation. The respondents could be divided into two groups. One stressed the importance of testing because it reveals the individual's current condition. Those who test negative are often motivated to change their behavior to avoid seroconverting; those who test positive can take steps to avoid spreading the virus. Another group opposed testing because there is no cure for AIDS. Their main question was, "What is the sense of getting tested if there is nothing you can do about it? It only fucks you up."

As a researcher, I had difficulty taking a stand on this issue. Generally I encouraged testing because of the respondents' involvement in risky behaviors.

Respondents who had tested positive for HIV antibodies wanted to discuss their status with me. Because we had already developed a relationship, they trusted me more than they would a "strange" counselor. Jacky, a 24-year-old street prostitute, confided in me: "I can't talk with them folks. They are straight or faggots and don't know what they are talking about. I don't need a preacher telling me what to do. They better get their own act together. I'm scared and don't want to die. What am I going to tell my old man?"

AIDS changed the relationship between me and my respondents. I began to be seen as a sort of on-the-stroll counselor, even though I did not have a lot to offer besides listening and trying to make appropriate referrals. I remember one case in particular: that of Micky and Jeanne.

Micky was 32 years old; his girlfriend Jeanne was 26. They both injected drugs and smoked crack. Micky went out and "did his thing" to get cash, and Jeanne turned tricks when he did not have enough money to support both of them. Then Micky started feeling sick. He was so tired he could not work. Jeanne started working more hours while a friend of Micky's watched her back in exchange for some dope. Jeanne, Micky, and I spent a lot of time together. One day he started asking questions about AIDS. He was going to see a doctor because he felt very sick.

Three days later Jeanne told me he was in the hospital. He got very sick and an ambulance had to pick him up. She did not know what to do. A week later Micky was out on the street again. He refused to sign a form and the hospital let him go as soon as he could walk. While in the hospital Micky was tested for AIDS; he tested positive. He did not want to talk with a counselor.

I tried to persuade Micky and Jeanne to seek help, but they felt that no one understood them. They also wanted to continue to get high, each with their own syringe. Micky said, "I'm going to die and I want to enjoy things. I can make that decision myself." In a few months, Micky died. Jeanne was never tested and went on working.

One of the ethical questions one faces as a researcher is what to do when an infected drug user continues to share hypodermic sets or an infected prostitute continues to have sex with her customers and/or boyfriend without using prophylactics. I frequently dealt with individuals who were seropositive but did not protect others against infection. One of them said to me, "They know as well as I do what the deal is. In this life everybody takes care of himself. If you want to take chances, it's your responsibility. I don't have to warn others."

My conversations with respondents about changing drug-using and sexual behaviors became more concrete as more people became sick and died of AIDS. The people who share a stroll or a copping area form a relatively closed community. Because of the visible effects of AIDS on members of the community, issues like drugs and sex came to be discussed more openly. Almost everybody I spoke with knew the ways in which the AIDS virus can be spread, and conversations about the use of condoms and the sharing of "works" became more common. Increasingly, I was not the person who brought up these issues. Respondents came up to me and asked me questions, or simply wanted to talk about what was going on. The threat posed by AIDS to almost everybody in the community made people more open. It also made them feel more vulnerable. It is scary to see your buddies get sick and die.

The increasing number of friends and acquaintances dying of AIDS affected me deeply. Attending funerals became a way of showing my concern and respect. In one brief period six people from one research site died. I had known four of them fairly well and had interviewed the other two. The latter were street prostitutes who used drugs intravenously; the others included a drug-using prostitute, a male hustler, and two intravenous drug users, one female and the other male. All had lived in close proximity and had frequent dealings with one another. The social linkages among them had been strong. Many of their friends had known all or some of them.

I was upset by the high rate of death among the people I was studying. I mentioned this to one of the women, who answered, "We all have this problem. It is going to get worse. Over half of the people around here are infected. Can you imagine . . . If you are out on the street long enough you learn to cope with everything. Getting sad or scared is not going to help. We have to survive. You have to set limits."

After this conversation I decided that things were getting out of hand. I discussed my feelings with several people, including colleagues and "field friends." In one neighborhood the situation had become so bad that children were referring to funeral cars as "AIDS wagons." But then something happened that made me realize that alongside of death there is always life.

A Hispanic woman, clearly ill, was trying to walk toward a nearby hospital. She was visibly pregnant. I approached her, and while we were talking her water broke. I realized that I didn't have time to get a car, so I jumped into the middle of the street and stopped the first car that came along. It was occupied by a middle-aged white couple. While I was explaining what was happening the woman groaned and said the baby, her second child, was coming. Although we were less than five minutes from the hospital, the baby was born in the back seat of the car. The woman in the front seat started crying and saying how thankful she was that we had chosen their car. The man walked away, sickened by the mess in the car. The mother, Carmen, cried and looked happily at her baby as she carried it into the hospital. I stood around, confused and disoriented. My clothes and hands were dirty. I was overwhelmed by having been involved in the birth of a baby on the same streets where people were dying of AIDS.

The AIDS epidemic has given ethnographic research a new dimension. AIDS has made me more aware of the fact that every researcher is affected by the work he or she does. One cannot remain neutral and uninvolved; even as an outsider, the researcher is part of the community under study and must recognize that fact.

QUESTIONS

1. What kind of sociological research do ethnographers like Claire Sterk do? How does it compare to other methods?
2. How does Sterk's research bear on the erroneous idea that AIDS is a "gay disease"?

Part II: Social Dynamics

STIGMA AND SOCIAL IDENTITY
Erving Goffman

Erving Goffman applied the interactionist perspective with a genius that is unsurpassed in the history of sociological research. Much of his writing delves into ideas of normality and deviance from the norms that define it. In this essay, he develops some ideas about the social concepts of identity and stigma. In other writings, he provides examples of how people interact in small groups or in couples to produce shared meanings about their places in society. Goffman is a master of the closely observed description of the microsocial world.

In his writing on stigma, Goffman shows how a person comes to share and accept the negative definitions imposed by others. He also describes how "normal" people define others as being stigmatized and how this definition reduces the stigmatized person's chances in life. In reading Goffman's work, it is helpful to try to think of your own examples. Sometimes he offers examples that are very brief or tucked into intriguing footnotes. At other times he develops extended and fascinating examples of the particular aspect of stigma that he is describing. You will find that if you read slowly and with enough care to supply examples from your own experience, his writing, which at first seems difficult, will become extremely compelling.

The Greeks, who were apparently strong on visual aids, originated the term *stigma* to refer to bodily signs designed to expose something unusual and bad about the moral status of the signifier. The signs were cut or burnt into the body and advertised that the bearer was a slave, a criminal, or a traitor—a blemished person, ritually polluted, to be avoided, especially in public places. Later, in Christian times, two layers of metaphor were added to the term: the first referred to bodily signs of holy grace that took the form of eruptive blossoms on the skin; the second, a medical allusion to this religious allusion, referred to bodily signs of physical disorder. Today the term is widely used in something like the original literal sense, but is applied more to the disgrace itself than to the bodily evidence of it. Furthermore, shifts have occurred in the kinds of disgrace that arouse concern. Students, however, have made little effort to describe the structural preconditions of stigma, or even to provide a definition of the concept itself. It seems necessary, therefore, to try at the beginning to sketch in some very general assumptions and definitions. . . .

Society establishes the means of categorizing persons and the complement of attributes felt to be ordinary and natural for members of each of these categories. Social settings establish the categories of persons likely to be encountered there. The routines of social intercourse in established settings allow us to deal with anticipated others without special attention or thought. When a stranger comes into our presence, then, first appearances are likely to enable us to anticipate his category and attributes, his "social identity"—to use a term that is better than "social status" because personal attributes such as "honesty" are involved, as well as structural ones, like "occupation."

We lean on these anticipations that we have, transforming them into normative expectations, into righteously presented demands.

Typically, we do not become aware that we have made these demands or aware of what they are until an active question arises as to whether or not they will be fulfilled. It is then that we are likely to realize that all along we had been making certain assumptions as to what the individual before us ought to be. Thus, the demands we make might better be called demands made "in effect," and the character we impute to the individual might better be seen as an imputation made in potential retrospect—a characterization "in effect," a *virtual social identity.* The category and attributes he could in fact be proved to possess will be called his *actual social identity.*

While the stranger is present before us, evidence can arise of his possessing an attribute that makes him different from others in the category of persons available for him to be, and of a less desirable kind—in the extreme, a person who is quite thoroughly bad, or dangerous, or weak. He is thus reduced in our minds from a whole and usual person to a tainted, discounted one. Such an attribute is a stigma, especially when its discrediting effect is very extensive; sometimes it is also called a failing, a shortcoming, a handicap. It constitutes a special discrepancy between virtual and actual social identity. Note that there are other types of discrepancy between virtual and actual social identity, for example the kind that causes us to reclassify an individual from one socially anticipated category to a different but equally well-anticipated one, and the kind that causes us to alter our estimation of the individual upward. Note, too, that not all undesirable attributes are at issue, but only those which are incongruous with our stereotype of what a given type of individual should be.

The term stigma, then, will be used to refer to an attribute that is deeply discrediting, but it should be seen that a language of relationships, not attributes, is really needed. An attribute that stigmatizes one type of possessor can confirm the usualness of another, and therefore is neither creditable nor discreditable as a thing in itself. For example, some jobs in America cause holders without the expected college education to conceal this fact; other jobs, however, can lead the few of their holders who have a higher education to keep this a secret, lest they be marked as failures and outsiders. Similarly, a middle class boy may feel no compunction in being seen going to the library; a professional criminal, however, writes:

> I can remember before now on more than one occasion, for instance, going into a public library near where I was living, and looking over my shoulder a couple of times before I actually went in just to make sure no one who knew me was standing about and seeing me do it.[1]

So, too, an individual who desires to fight for his country may conceal a physical defect, lest his claimed physical status be discredited; later, the same individual, embittered and trying to get out of the army, may succeed in gaining admission to the army hospital, where he would be discredited if discovered in not really having an acute sickness.[2] A stigma, then, is really a special kind of relationship between attribute and stereotype, although I don't propose to continue to say so, in part because there are important attributes that almost everywhere in our society are discrediting.

The term stigma and its synonyms conceal a double perspective: does the stigmatized individual assume his differentness is known about already or is evident on the spot, or does he assume it is neither known about by those present nor immediately perceivable by them? In the first case one deals with the plight of the *discredited,* in the second with that of the *discreditable.* This is an important difference, even though a particular stigmatized individual is likely to have experience with both situations. I will begin with the situation of the discredited and move on to the discreditable but not always separate the two.

Three grossly different types of stigma may be mentioned. First there are abominations of the body—the various physical deformities. Next there are blemishes of individual character perceived as weak will, domineering or unnatural passions, treacherous and rigid beliefs, and dishonesty, these being inferred from a known record of, for example, mental disorder, imprisonment, addiction, alcoholism, homosexuality, unemployment, suicidal attempts, and radical political behavior. Finally there are the tribal stigma of race, nation, and religion, these being stigma that can be transmitted through lineages and equally contaminate all members of a family.[3] In all of these various instances of stigma, however, including those the Greeks had in mind, the same sociological features are found: an individual who might have been received easily in ordinary social

[1]T. Parker and R. Allerton, *The Courage of His Convictions* (London: Hutchinson & Co., 1962), p. 109.

[2]In this connection see the review by M. Meltzer, "Countermanipulation through Malingering," in A. Biderman and H. Zimmer, eds., *The Manipulation of Human Behavior* (New York: John Wiley & Sons, 1961), pp. 277–304.

[3]In recent history, especially in Britain, low class status functioned as an important tribal stigma, the sins of the parents, or at least their milieu, being visited on the child, should the child rise improperly far above his initial station. The management of class stigma is of course a central theme in the English novel.

intercourse possesses a trait that can obtrude itself upon attention and turn those of us whom he meets away from him, breaking the claim that his other attributes have on us. He possesses a stigma, an undesired differentness from what we had anticipated. We and those who do not depart negatively from the particular expectations at issue I shall call the *normals.*

The attitudes we normals have toward a person with a stigma, and the actions we take in regard to him, are well known, since these responses are what benevolent social action is designed to soften and ameliorate. By definition, of course, we believe the person with a stigma is not quite human. On this assumption we exercise varieties of discrimination, through which we effectively, if often unthinkingly, reduce his life chances. We construct a stigma-theory, an ideology to explain his inferiority and account for the danger he represents, sometimes rationalizing an animosity based on other differences, such as those of social class.[4] We use specific stigma terms such as cripple, bastard, moron in our daily discourse as a source of metaphor and imagery, typically without giving thought to the original meaning.[5] We tend to impute a wide range of imperfections on the basis of the original one,[6] and at the same time to impute some desirable but undesired attributes, often of a supernatural cast, such as "sixth sense," or "understanding":[7]

> For some, there may be a hesitancy about touching or steering the blind, while for others, the perceived failure to see may be generalized into a gestalt of disability, so that the individual shouts at the blind as if they were deaf or attempts to lift them as if they were crippled. Those confronting the blind may have a whole range of belief that is anchored in the stereotype. For instance, they may think they are subject to unique judgment, assuming the blinded individual draws on special channels of information unavailable to others.[8]

Further, we may perceive his defensive response to his situation as a direct expression of his defect, and then see both defect and response as just retribution for something he or his parents or his tribe did, and hence a justification of the way we treat him.[9]

Now turn from the normal to the person he is normal against. It seems generally true that members of a social category may strongly support a standard of judgment that they and others agree does not directly apply to them. Thus it is that a businessman may demand womanly behavior from females or ascetic behavior from monks, and not construe himself as someone who ought to realize either of these styles of conduct. The distinction is between realizing a norm and merely supporting it. The issue of stigma does not arise here, but only where there is some expectation on all sides that those in a given category should not only support a particular norm but also realize it.

Also, it seems possible for an individual to fail to live up to what we effectively demand of him, and yet be relatively untouched by this failure; insulated by his alienation, protected by identity beliefs of his own, he feels that he is a full-fledged normal human being, and that we are the ones who are not quite human. He bears a stigma but does not seem to be impressed or repentant about doing so. This possibility is celebrated in exemplary tales about Mennonites, Gypsies, shameless scoundrels, and very orthodox Jews.

In America at present, however, separate systems of honor seem to be on the decline. The stigmatized individual tends to hold the same beliefs about identity that we do; this is a pivotal fact. His deepest feelings about what he is may be his sense of being a "normal person," a human being like anyone else, a person, therefore, who deserves a fair chance and a fair break.[10] (Actually, however phrased, he bases his claims not on what he

[4]D. Riesman, "Some Observations Concerning Marginality," *Phylon,* Second Quarter, 1951, 122.

[5]The case regarding mental patients is presented by T. J. Scheff in a forthcoming paper.

[6]In regard to the blind, see E. Henrich and L. Kriegel, eds., *Experiments in Survival* (New York: Association for the Aid of Crippled Children, 1961), pp. 152 and 186; and H. Chevigny, *My Eyes Have a Cold Nose* (New Haven, Conn.: Yale University Press, paperbound, 1962), p. 201.

[7]In the words of one blind woman, "I was asked to endorse a perfume, presumably because being sightless my sense of smell was super-discriminating." See T. Keitlen (with N. Lobsenz), *Farewell to Fear* (New York: Avon, 1962), p. 10.

[8]A. G. Gowman, *The War Blind in American Social Structure* (New York: American Foundation for the Blind, 1957), p. 198.

[9]For examples, see Macgregor *et al., op. cit.,* throughout.

[10]The notion of "normal human being" may have its source in the medical approach to humanity or in the tendency of large-scale bureaucratic organizations, such as the nation state, to treat all members in some respects as equal. Whatever its origins, it seems to provide the basic imagery through which laymen currently conceive of themselves. Interestingly, a convention seems to have emerged in popular life-story writing where a questionable person proves his claim to normalcy by citing his acquisition of a spouse and children, and, oddly, by attesting to his spending Christmas and Thanksgiving with them.

thinks is due *everyone,* but only everyone of a selected social category into which he unquestionably fits, for example, anyone of his age, sex, profession, and so forth.) Yet he may perceive, usually quite correctly, that whatever others profess, they do not really "accept" him and are not ready to make contact with him on "equal grounds."[11] Further, the standards he has incorporated from the wider society equip him to be intimately alive to what others see as his failing, inevitably causing him, if only for moments, to agree that he does indeed fall short of what he really ought to be. Shame becomes a central possibility, arising from the individual's perception of one of his own attributes as being a defiling thing to possess, and one he can readily see himself as not possessing.

The immediate presence of normals is likely to reinforce this split between self-demands and self, but in fact self-hate and self-derogation can also occur when only he and a mirror are about:

> When I got up at last . . . and had learned to walk again, one day I took a hand glass and went to a long mirror to look at myself, and I went alone. I didn't want anyone . . . to know how I felt when I saw myself for the first time. But there was no noise, no outcry; I didn't scream with rage when I saw myself. I just felt numb. That person in the mirror *couldn't* be me. I felt inside like a healthy, ordinary, lucky person—oh, not like the one in the mirror! Yet when I turned my face to the mirror there were my own eyes looking back, hot with shame . . . when I did not cry or make any sound, it became impossible that I should speak of it to anyone, and the confusion and the panic of my discovery were locked inside me then and there, to be faced alone, for a very long time to come.[12]

> Over and over I forgot what I had seen in the mirror. It could not penetrate into the interior of my mind and become an integral part of me. I felt as if it had nothing to do with me; it was only a disguise. But it was not the kind of disguise which is put on voluntarily by the person who wears it, and which is intended to confuse other people as to one's identity. My disguise had been put on me without my consent or knowledge like the ones in fairy tales, and it was I myself who was confused by it, as to my own identity. I looked in the mirror, and was horror-struck because I did not recognize myself. In the place where I was standing, with that persistent romantic elation in me, as if I were a favored fortunate person to whom everything was possible, I saw a stranger, a little, pitiable, hideous figure, and a face that became, as I stared at it, painful and blushing with shame. It was only a disguise, but it was on me, for life. It was there, it was there, it was real. Every one of those encounters was like a blow on the head. They left me dazed and dumb and senseless everytime, until slowly and stubbornly my robust persistent illusion of well-being and of personal beauty spread all through me again, and I forgot the irrelevant reality and was all unprepared and vulnerable again.[13]

The central feature of the stigmatized individual's situation in life can now be stated. It is a question of what is often, if vaguely, called "acceptance." Those who have dealings with him fail to accord him the respect and regard which the uncontaminated aspects of his social identity have led them to anticipate extending, and have led him to anticipate receiving; he echoes this denial by finding that some of his own attributes warrant it.

QUESTIONS

1. Cite an example from this essay that demonstrates Erving Goffman's interactionist perspective.
2. Why might stigmatized people sometimes turn to other types of deviant behavior as well?

[11]A criminal's view of this nonacceptance is presented in Parker and Allerton, *op. cit.,* pp. 110–111.

[12]K. B. Hathaway, *The Little Locksmith* (New York: Coward-McCann, 1943), p. 41, in Wright, *op. cit.,* p. 157.

[13]*Ibid.,* pp. 46–47. For general treatments of the self-disliking sentiments, see K. Lewin, *Resolving Social Conflicts,* Part III (New York: Harper & Row, 1948); A. Kardiner and L. Ovesey, *The Mark of Oppression: A Psychosocial Study of the American Negro* (New York: W. W. Norton & Company, 1951); and E. H. Erikson, *Childhood and Society* (New York: W. W. Norton & Company, 1950).

WHO THEY ARE AND WHY THEY COME

Alejandro Portes and Rubén C. Rumbaut

The new waves of immigration to the United States are rapidly changing the social landscape of many metropolitan regions. The United States has always prided itself on being a diverse nation where the people of the world converge in search of opportunity and the freedom to realize their dreams. In recent years, however, the sheer volume of immigration to some areas, especially southern California, Florida, and the Northeast, has given rise to fears of job competition in some segments of the population. Ethnocentric people may resent the immigrants' "foreignness" and their initial failure to conform to conventional codes of dress or speech. These reactions are particularly noticeable in regions where there are relatively few immigrants. In the nation's larger urban centers, where generations of immigration have produced culturally diverse populations, there tends to be more tolerance and understanding of newcomers, but there too conflicts are common.

Sociologists Alejandro Portes and Rubén Rumbaut are among the nation's most respected scholars focusing on the new immigration. Their work, as represented in this essay, presents empirical data about the new immigrant groups. The sociological knowledge they provide helps readers get beyond the stereotypes. Their work also explores the impact of immigration on the regions and communities where the new immigrants settle. From immigrant families themselves, the authors draw upon the strengths of their personal and sociological backgrounds to select the most telling examples and situations in exploring the nature of the experience of settling into a new and vibrant society.

In Guadalajara, Juan Manuel Fernández worked as a mechanic in his uncle's repair shop making the equivalent of $150 per month. At thirty-two and after ten years on the job, he decided it was time to go into business on his own. The family, his uncle included, was willing to help, but capital for the new venture was scarce. Luisa, Juan's wife, owned a small corner grocery shop; when money ran out at the end of the month, she often fed the family off the store's shelves. The store was enough to sustain her and her children but not to capitalize her husband's project. For a while, it looked as if Juan would remain a worker for life.

Today Juan owns his own auto repair shop, where he employs three other mechanics, two Mexicans and a Salvadoran. The shop is not in Guadalajara, however, but in Gary, Indiana. The entire family—Luisa, the two children, and a brother—have resettled there. Luisa does not work any longer because she does not speak English and because income from her husband's business is enough to support the family. The children attend school and already speak better English than their parents. They resist the idea of going back to Mexico.

Juan crossed the border on his own near El Paso in 1979. No one stopped him, and he was able to head north toward a few distant cousins and the prospect of a factory job. To his surprise, he found one easily and at the end of four months was getting double the minimum wage in steady employment. Almost every worker in the plant was Mexican, his foreman was Puerto Rican, and the language of work was uniformly Spanish. Three trips from Gary to Guadalajara during the next two years persuaded him that it made much better sense to move his business project north of the border. Guadalajara was teeming with repair shops of all sorts, and competition was fierce. "In Gary," he said, "many Mexicans would not get their cars fixed because they did not know how to bargain with an American mechanic." Sensing the opportunity, he cut remittances to Mexico and opened a local savings account instead.

During his last trip, the "migra" (border patrol) stopped him shortly after crossing; that required a costly second attempt two days later with a hired "coyote" (smuggler). The incident put a stop to the commuting. Juan started fixing cars out of a shed in front of his barrio home. Word got around that there was a reliable Spanish-speaking mechanic in the neighborhood. In a few months, he was able to rent an abandoned garage, buy some equipment, and eventually hire others. To stay in business, Juan has had to obtain a municipal permit and pay a fee. He pays his workers in cash, however, and neither deducts taxes from their wages nor contributes to Social Security for them. All transactions are informal and, for the most part, in cash.

Juan and Luisa feel a great deal of nostalgia for Mexico, and both firmly intend to return. "In this country, we've been able to move ahead economically, but it is not our own," she says. "The gringos will always consider us inferior." Their savings are not in the bank, as before the shop was rented, but in land in Guadalajara, a small house for his parents, and the goodwill of many relatives who receive periodic remittances. They figure that in ten years they will be able to return, although they worry about their children, who may be thoroughly Americanized by then. A more pressing problem is their lack of "papers" and the constant threat of deportation. Juan has devised ingenious ways to run the business, despite his illegal status, but it is a constant problem. A good part of his recent earnings is in the hands of an immigration lawyer downtown, who has promised to obtain papers for a resident's visa, so far without results.

At age twenty-six, Nguyen Van Tran was a young lieutenant in the army of the Republic of South Vietnam when a strategic retreat order from the ARVN high command quickly turned into the final rout. Nguyen spent three years in Communist reeducation camps, all the while attempting to conceal his past as a skilled electronics technician. He finally got aboard a boat bound for Malaysia and after two more years in a refugee camp arrived in Los Angeles in 1980. He had neither family nor friends in the city, but the government provided some resettlement aid and the opportunity to improve his English. At the end of a year, he had secured a job in a local electronics assembly plant, which brought in enough to support himself and his wife and child.

Seeing this plant double in a single year, Nguyen realized the opportunities opening up in electronics. He enrolled in the local community college at night and graduated with an associate degree in computer science. He pooled his savings with another Vietnamese technician and a Chinese engineer and in 1983 launched his own firm. Two years later Integrated Circuits, Inc., employed approximately three hundred workers; most were not Asians, but undocumented Mexican women. In 1985, the company sold about $20 million worth of semiconductors and other equipment to the local IBM plant and other large firms. ICI has even started its own line of IBM-compatible personal computers, the Trantex, which has sold well so far in the local market.

Nguyen, who is chairman of the company, sports a mustache, a sleek Mercedes, and a brand-new name, George Best. Perhaps for fear of the "protection gangs" re-created by former Vietnamese policemen in Los Angeles, he has kept a low profile within the Vietnamese community. The name change is part of this approach. "Mr. Best" is not particularly nationalistic, nor does he dream of returning to Vietnam. He attributes his remarkable five-year ascent to hard work and a willingness to take risks. To underline the point, he has hung a large portrait of himself in his community college graduation gown behind his oversized desk. He and his wife are already U.S. citizens. They vote Republican, and he has recently joined the local chamber of commerce.

Lilia González-Fleites left Cuba at fifteen, sent alone by her formerly wealthy parents, who remained behind. The Catholic Welfare Agency received her in Miami, and she went to live with other refugee children in an orphanage in Kendall, Florida, until released to an aunt. She finished high school promptly and married, without her parents' consent, her boyfriend from Cuba, Tomás. There was little work in Miami, and the young couple accepted an offer from the Cuban Refugee Center to resettle them, along with the rest of Tomás's family, in North Carolina. Everyone found work in the tobacco and clothing factories except Lilia, whom Tomás kept at home. At eighteen, the formerly pampered girl found herself a cook and maid for Tomás's entire family.

By sheer luck, the same order of nuns who ran her private school in Havana had a college nearby. Lilia used her school connections to gain admittance with a small scholarship and found herself a part-time job.

Those were hard years, working in one city and attending school in another. Tomás and Lilia rarely saw each other because he also decided to return to school while still working.

At age thirty-nine, Lilia is today a successful Miami architect. Divorced from Tomás, she has not remarried, instead pursuing her professional career with single-minded determination. When Cuban refugees finally abandoned their dreams of return, Lilia entered local politics, affiliating with the Republican party. She ran for state office in 1986 but was defeated. Undaunted, she remains active in the party and has become increasingly prominent in south Florida political circles. More than an immigrant success story, she sees herself at the beginning of a public career that will bridge the gap between the Anglo and Cuban communities in south Florida. Her unaccented English, fierce loyalty to her adopted country, and ability to shift easily between languages and cultures bodes well for her political future. She will run again in 1988.

After finishing medical school, Amitar Ray confronted the prospect of working *ad honorem* in one of the few well-equipped hospitals in Bombay or moving to a job in the countryside and to quick obsolescence in his career. He opted instead for preparing and taking the Educational Council for Foreign Medical Graduates (ECFMG) examinations, administered at the local branch of the Indo-American Cultural Institute. He passed it on his second attempt. In 1972, there was a shortage of doctors in the United States and U.S. consulates were directed to facilitate the emigration of qualified physicians from abroad.

Amitar and his wife, also a doctor, had little difficulty obtaining permanent residents' visas under the third preference of the U.S. immigration law, reserved for professionals of exceptional ability. He went on to specialize in anesthesiology and completed his residence at a public hospital in Brooklyn. After four years, nostalgia and the hope that things had improved at home moved the Rays to go back to India with their young daughter, Rita. The trip strengthened their professional and family ties, but it also dispelled any doubts as to where their future was. Medical vacancies were rare and paid a fraction of what he earned as a resident in Brooklyn. More important, there were few opportunities to grow professionally because he would have had to combine several part-time jobs to earn a livelihood, leaving little time for study.

At fifty-one, Amitar is now associate professor of anesthesiology at a midwestern medical school; his wife has a local practice as an internist. Their combined income is in the six figures, affording them a very comfortable life-style. Their daughter is a senior at Bryn Mawr, and she plans to pursue a graduate degree in international relations. There are few Indian immigrants in the mid-sized city where the Rays live; thus, they have had to learn local ways in order to gain entry into American social circles. Their color is sometimes a barrier to close contact with white middle-class families, but they have cultivated many friendships among the local faculty and medical community.

Ties to India persist and are strengthened through periodic trips and the professional help the Rays are able to provide to colleagues back home. They have already sponsored the immigration of two bright young physicians from their native city. More important, they make sure that information on new medical developments is relayed to a few selected specialists back home. However, there is little chance that they will return, even after retirement. Work and new local ties play a role in this, but the decisive factor is a thoroughly Americanized daughter whose present life and future have very little to do with India. Rita does not plan to marry soon; she is interested in Latin American politics, and her current goal is a career in the foreign service.

After a lapse of half a century, the United States has again become a country of immigration. In 1980, the foreign-born population reached 14.1 million or 6.2 percent of the total. Although a far cry from the situation sixty years earlier, when immigrants accounted for 13.2 percent of the American population, the impact of contemporary immigration is both significant and growing. Numerous books and articles have called attention to this revival and sought its causes—first in a booming American economy and second in the liberalized provisions of the 1965 immigration act. A common exercise is to compare this "new" immigration with the "old" inflow at the turn of the century. Similarities include the predominantly urban destination of most newcomers, their concentration in a few port cities, and their willingness to accept the lowest paid jobs. Differences are more frequently stressed, however, for the "old" immigration was overwhelmingly European and white; but the present inflow is, to a large extent, nonwhite and comes from countries of the Third World.

The public image of contemporary immigration has been colored to a large extent by the Third World origins of most recent arrivals. Because the sending countries are generally poor, many Americans believe that the immigrants themselves are uniformly poor and uneducated. Their move is commonly portrayed as a one-way escape from hunger, want, and persecution and their arrival on U.S. shores as not too different from that of the tired, "huddled masses" that Emma Lazarus immortalized at the base of the Statue of Liberty. The "quality" of the newcomers and their chances for assimilation are sometimes portrayed as worse because of their non-European past and the precarious legal status of many.

The reality is very different. The four previous cases, each a composite of real-life experiences, are certainly not representative of all recent immigrants. Clearly, not all newcomers are doctors or skilled mechanics, and fewer still become politicians or millionaires. Still, these are not isolated instances. Underneath its apparent uniformity, contemporary immigration features a bewildering variety of origins, return patterns, and modes of adaptation to American society. Never before has the United States received immigrants from so many countries, from such different social and economic backgrounds, and for so many reasons. Although pre–World War I European immigration was by no means homogeneous, the differences between successive waves of Irish, Italians, Jews, Greeks, and Poles often pale by comparison with the current diversity. For the same reason, theories coined in the wake of the Europeans' arrival at the turn of the century have been made obsolete by events during the last decades.

Increasingly implausible, for example, is the view of a uniform assimilation process that different groups undergo in the course of several generations as a precondition for their social and economic advancement. There are today first-generation millionaires who speak broken English, foreign-born mayors of large cities, and top-flight immigrant engineers and scientists in the nation's research centers; there are also those, at the other extreme, who cannot even take the first step toward assimilation because of the insecurity linked to an uncertain legal status. . . .

Many of the countries from which today's immigrants come have one of their largest cities in the United States. Los Angeles' Mexican population is next in size to Mexico City, Monterrey, and Guadalajara. Havana is not much larger than Cuban Miami, and Santo Domingo holds a precarious advantage over Dominican New York. This is not the case for all groups; others, such as Asian Indians, Laotians, Argentines, and Brazilians, are more dispersed throughout the country. Reasons for both these differences and other characteristics of contemporary immigrant groups are not well known—in part because of the recency of their arrival and in part because of the common expectation that their assimilation process would conform to the well-known European pattern. But immigrant America is a different place today from the America that emerged out of Ellis Island and grew up in the tenements of New York and Boston.

QUESTIONS

1. According to Alejandro Portes and Rubén G. Rumbaut, how does the "new immigration" to the United States differ from earlier immigration?

2. What does it mean when we say that immigrants are distributed unevenly throughout the United States?

Part III: Social Divisions

THE CORPORATE RICH

C. W. Mills

C. W. Mills is perhaps the most commonly cited "critical" sociologist in American social thought. A Columbia University professor who died in 1962, Mills is well known for his descriptions of the sociological imagination and his penetrating research on the American class system. This essay is from his book The Power Elite, *a work that combined research and theory into an analysis of the way powerful men in the defense establishment, corporations, and politics worked together to foster the class interests of themselves and others like them—to the detriment, according to Mills, of the majority of Americans.*

During the tumultuous 1960s, The Power Elite *became a best-selling sociological critique of American society. Although Mills did not accept all the theories and predictions of classical Marxism, he was a radical in that he believed poor and working-class people needed to understand that their class interests were opposed to those of the rich and powerful.* The Power Elite *attempts to show that, contrary to what many Americans have always believed, there is a "ruling class" in the United States and that its "power elite" acts in a way that profoundly shapes the lives of most Americans. Does the nation fight wars in which the children of working-class and poor people make the most sacrifices? Are laws passed that favor the rich at the expense of the poor? Does government generally act in favor of those who are already well off? These are the kinds of pointed and critical questions posed by Mills.*

Many of the numbers Mills cites in this essay are now out of date, but the relationships among them—between wealth and tax policies, for example—remain extremely current. Indeed, Chapter 12 of the text shows that, as Mills might have predicted, the proportion of wealth in the hands of relatively few individuals and families in the United States has continued to increase in the last fifteen or twenty years. But are the corporate rich part of a more sinister "power elite" that runs the nation? This is still an extremely controversial notion and one that sociologists have not ever agreed upon. In the post–Cold War period many sociologists would argue that the influence of the military has diminished, and although the corporate rich have an inordinate amount of power, the evidence that they form a power elite is somewhat sketchy. Still, the contours of American class stratification explored in Mills's essay remain a fruitful area of sociological research, especially among those who do not accept the status quo but are critical of the extremes of wealth and poverty in the United States and other affluent nations.

The old-fashioned rich were simply the propertied classes, organized on a family basis and seated in a locality, usually a big city. The corporate rich, in addition to such people, include those whose high "incomes" include the privileges and prerogatives that have come to be features of high executive position. The corporate rich thus includes members of the big-city rich of the metropolitan 400, of the national rich who possess the great American fortunes, as well as chief executives of the major corporations. The propertied class, in the age of corporate property, has become a corporate rich, and in becoming corporate has consolidated its power and drawn to its defense new men of more executive and more political stance. Its members have become self-conscious in terms of the corporate world they represent. As men of status they have secured their privileges and prerogatives in the most stable private institutions of American society. They are a corporate rich because they depend directly, as well as indirectly, for their money, their privileges, their securities, their advantages, their powers on the world of the big corporations. All the old-fashioned rich are now more or less of the corporate rich, and the newer types of privileged men are there with them. In fact, no one can become rich or stay rich in America today without becoming involved, in one way or another, in the world of the corporate rich.

During the 'forties and 'fifties the national shape of the income distribution became less a pyramid with a flat base than a fat diamond with a bulging middle. Taking into account price changes and tax increases, proportionately more families in 1929 than in 1951 (from 65 to 46 per cent) received family incomes of less than $3,000; fewer then than now received between $3,000 and $7,500 (from 29 to 47 per cent); but about the same proportions (6 and 7 per cent) in both 1929 and 1951 received $7,500 or more.

Many economic forces at work during the war, and the war-preparations boom that has followed it, have made some people on the very bottom levels rise into what used to be the middle-range income levels, and some of those who used to be in the middle-range of income levels became upper-middle or upper. The changed distribution of real income has thus affected the middle and lower levels of the population, with which, of course, we are not here directly concerned. Our interest is in the higher levels; and the forces at work on the income structure have not changed the decisive facts of the big money.

At the very top of the mid-century American economy, there are some 120 people who each year receive a million dollars or more. Just below them, another 379 people appropriate between a half a million and a million. Some 1,383 people get from $250,000 to $499,999. And below all these, there is the broader base of 11,490 people who receive from $100,000 to $249,999.

Altogether, then, in 1949, there were 13,822 people who declared incomes of $100,000 or more to the tax collector. Let us draw the line of the openly declared corporate rich at that level: $100,000 a year and up. It is not an entirely arbitrary figure. For there is one fact about the fat diamond that remains true regardless of how many people are on each of its levels: on the middle and higher levels especially, the greater the yearly income, the greater the proportion of it from property, and the smaller the proportion from salaries, entrepreneurial withdrawal, or wages. The rich of the higher incomes, in short, are still of the propertied class. The lower incomes derive from wages.

One hundred thousand dollars a year is the income level on which property enters the income picture in a major way: two-thirds (67 per cent) of the money received by the 13,702 people in the declared $100,000 and up to $999,999 bracket comes from property—from dividends, capital gains, estates, and trusts. The remaining one-third is split between chief executives and top entrepreneurs.

The higher you go into these upper reaches, the more does property count, and the less does income for services performed. Thus 94 per cent of the money of the 120 people receiving a million dollars or more in 1949 came from property; 5 per cent from entrepreneurial profits, 1 per cent from salaries. Among these 120 people, there was considerable variation in the type of property from which their money came. But, regardless of the legal arrangements involved, those with big incomes receive it overwhelmingly from corporate property. That is the first reason that all the rich are now corporate rich, and that is the key economic difference between the rich and the more than 99 per cent of the population who are well below the $100,000 income level.

In these tax-declared high-income classes, people come and go; every year the exact number of people varies. In 1929, when taxes were not so high as to make it so dangerous as now to declare high incomes, there were about 1,000 more such declarations than in 1949—a total of 14,816 declared incomes of $100,000 or more. In 1948 there were 16,280; in 1939 only 2,921. But on the highest levels there remains throughout the years a hard core of the very wealthy. Four-fifths of the 75 people who appropriated one million dollars or more in 1924, for example, got one million or more in at least one other year between 1917 and 1936. The chances are good that those who make it in one year will make it in another year or two. Farther down the pyramid, only 3 or 4 per cent of the population during the decade after World War II have held as much as $10,000 in liquid assets.

Since virtually all statistics of income are based on declarations to tax collectors, they do not fully reveal the "income" differences between the corporate rich and other Americans. In fact, one major difference has to do with privileges that are deliberately created for the exclusion of "income" from tax records. These privileges are so pervasive that we find it hard to take seriously the great publicity given to the "income revolution," which is said to have taken place over the last twenty years. A change, as we have just reported, has taken place in the total income distribution of the United States; but we do not find it very convincing to judge from declared income tax records that the share the rich receive of all the wealth in the country has decreased.

Tax rates being high, the corporate rich are quite nimble in figuring out ways to get income, or the things and experiences that income provides, in such a way as to escape taxation. The manner in which the corporate rich pay their taxes is more flexible and provides more opportunities for shrewd interpretations of the law than is true for the middle and lower classes. People of higher income figure their own tax deductions, or more usually have them figured by the experts they hire. Perhaps those whose income derives from property or from entrepreneurial and professional practice are as honest—or as dishonest—as poorer people on wages and salary, but they are also economically bolder, they have greater opportunities and greater skill, and, even more importantly, they have access to the very best skills available for such matters: accomplished lawyers and skillful accountants who specialize in taxation as a science and a game. In the nature of the case, it would be impossible to prove with exactitude, but it is difficult not to believe that as a general rule the higher the income and the more varied its sources, the greater the likelihood of the shrewd tax return. Much declared money is tricked, legally and illegally, from the tax collector; much illegal money is simply not declared.

Perhaps the most important tax loophole in retaining current income is the long-term capital gain. When a military man writes a best-seller or has it written for him, when a businessman sells his farm or a dozen pigs, when an executive sells his stock—the profit received is not considered as income but as capital gain, which means that the profit to the individual after taxes is approximately twice what it would have been if that same amount of money had been received as a salary or a dividend. Individuals claiming long-term capital gains pay taxes on only 50 per cent of that gain. The half that is taxed is taxed at a progressive rate applicable to a person's total income; but the maximum tax on such gains is 52 per cent. This means that at no time can the tax paid on these capital gains be more than 26 per cent of the total gain received; and it will be smaller if the total income, including the gain, leaves the individual in a lower income tax bracket. But when the flow of money is turned around the other way, a capital *loss* of over $1,000 (those under $1,000 may be deducted from ordinary income) can be spread backward or forward in a five-year span to offset capital gains.

Aside from capital gains, the most profitable tax loophole is perhaps the "depletion allowance" on oil and gas wells and mineral deposits. From 5 to $27\frac{1}{2}$ per cent of the gross income received on an oil well, but not exceeding 50 per cent of the net income from the property, is tax-free each year. Moreover, all the costs of drilling and developing an oil well can be deducted as they occur—instead of being capitalized and depreciated over the years of the well's productive life. The important point of privilege has less to do with the percentage allowed than with the continuation of the device long after the property is fully depreciated.

Those with enough money to play around may also off-set taxes by placing money in tax-free municipal bonds; they may split their income among various family members so that the taxes paid are at a lower rate than the combined income would have required. The rich cannot give away to friends or relatives more than a lifetime total of $30,000 plus $3,000 each year without paying a gift tax; although, in the name of both husband and wife, a couple can give twice that amount. The rich man can also make a tax-deductible gift (up to 20 per cent of yearly income that is given to recognized charities is not taxed as income) that will provide him security for the rest of his life. He can donate to a named charity the principal of a fund, but continue to receive the income from it. He thus makes an immediate deduction on his income tax return; and he cuts that part of his estate that is subject to inheritance taxes.

There are other techniques that help the rich preserve their money after they are dead in spite of high estate taxes. For example, it is possible to set up a trust for a grandchild, and stipulate that the *child* receive the income from the trust as long as he is alive, although the property legally belongs to the grandchild. It is only at the death of the child (instead of both the original owner *and* the child) that an estate tax is paid.

A family trust saves taxes—both current income tax and estate tax levied upon death—for income of the trust fund is taxed separately. In addition, the trust provides the property holder with continuous professional management, eliminates the worries of responsibility, keeps the property intact in one manageable sum, builds the strongest possible legal safeguards to property, and, in effect, enables the owner to continue to control his property after he is dead. . . .

For virtually every law taxing big money, there is a way those with big money can avoid it or minimize it. But such legal and illegal maneuvers are only part of the income privileges of the corporate rich: working hand-in-hand with the rules and regulations of the government, the corporations find ways directly to supplement the income of the executive rich. These various forms of feathering the nest now make it possible for executive members of the corporate rich to live richly on seemingly moderate incomes, while paying taxes lower than the law seemingly intends as fair and just. Among such privileged arrangements are [the] following:

Under the deferred pay contract, the corporation signs up for a given salary for a number of years, and further agrees to pay an annual retainer after retirement as long as the executive doesn't go to work for any competing firm. The executive's loyalty is thus linked to the company, and he is able to spread his income into the years when lower earnings will result in reduced taxes. One Chrysler executive, for example, recently signed a contract yielding him $300,000 a year for the next five years, then $75,000 a year for the rest of his life. A recently retired Chairman of U.S. Steel's Board, who was receiving a $211,000 salary, now gets $14,000 a year as his pension, plus $55,000 a year in "deferred pay."

Executives are given restricted options to buy stock at or below current market value. This keeps the executive with the company; for he is able to pick up the option only after a specified period of time such as a year, or he may only be able to use it to buy limited quantities of stock over a longer period of time—say five years. To the executive as riskless entrepreneur, at the time he picks up his option, there comes an immediate profit (the difference between the option price previously set and the market value of the stock at the time when he buys it). Most of the profit he makes if he later sells the stock is not considered taxable income by an obliging government: it is taxed at the lower capital gains rate. Nothing prevents him from borrowing money to pick up his option, and then selling the stock in six months at the higher market value. For example, in 1954, the president of an aircraft company was given—in salary, bonus, and pension credits—about $150,000, but after taxes he took home only about $75,000. However, if he wished to sell the 10,000 shares of stock he had bought on his company's option plan several months before, he could, after paying all taxes due, have also taken home $594,375. About one out of six companies listed on the New York Stock Exchange gave stock options to executives within a year or so after the 1950 tax law made them attractive as capital gains. Since then, the practice has spread.

QUESTIONS

1. Why do you think C. W. Mills is known as a critical sociologist? Is his power elite theory a critical theory? Why?

2. Mills wrote *The Power Elite* in the 1960s. Many of the income figures he cites are now out of date. If that is the case, why is the book still a valuable source of information about social stratification in the United States?

THE CHANGING WORLD MAP OF POVERTY

Peter Townsend

Peter Townsend is a British sociologist who is widely recognized as one of the world's leading experts on the comparative aspects of global poverty. His many books and articles about poverty in the industrialized and developing nations have been consulted by policymakers in the United Nations and other agencies that address the problems of poverty and inequality.

Like many sociologists who conduct research on poverty, Townsend wishes to show that there are important differences in the structural origins of poverty in rich and poor nations. Structural explanations usually refer to major features of social structure or changes in social structures that have far-reaching consequences for individuals, families, and communities. The loss of better-paying manufacturing jobs in the industrialized nations of the Northern Hemisphere, for example, is a structural change that has widened the gap between the rich and the poor in the more affluent nations. Political instability in many of the world's poorest nations, like Somalia or Rwanda, is a very different kind of social change, but it is also structural in that the political chaos in these nations derives from extreme weaknesses in the structure and stability of political institutions. These weaknesses, in turn, can lead to further impoverishment of the population and increased conflict and violence.

Townsend is committed to seeking policies that will address the causes and consequences of world poverty. His refusal to merely explain the status quo of extreme poverty or relative deprivation puts him in the category of sociologists who not only present research on inequality but also actively seek political solutions.

Our capacity to deal with poverty depends on giving equal and simultaneous attention to meaning, measurement, explanation and policy analysis. Table 1 illustrates the varied pattern requiring explanation. Poverty is not the same as inequality. Although the two have to be distinguished, they are connected. In the present state of knowledge it is easier to compare sections of the population, regions and countries on some measured interpretation of resources or income than it is on some measured interpretation of poverty. Although major improvements still remain to be made to the former it satisfies some of the requirements of consistency. The latter is more problematic, as readers will find. A measure of poverty must apply not just to the low end of the resource or income distribution, but must also involve the selection of criteria applying to a threshold of income at which needs are not met or there is a disproportionate risk of severe or multiple deprivation.

Table 1 also illustrates another key feature of the poverty analysis in this book. In dealing with the international statistics of poverty the differences *between* populations but also *within* populations have to be expressed. An acceptable theory of one has to be an acceptable theory of the other too. How can the pattern of world poverty be explained? The difference between rich and poor countries in command over income is vast. More than 160 countries are now listed in the information provided routinely by UN agencies. In allowing for variations in size, differences in aggregate income are usually expressed per person. For the countries of western and northern Europe, North America and some of the strongest oil-powers of the Middle East the average person's income, when standardised according to exchange rates, is as much as 50 times that found in the countries of the Far East, like India, Pakistan and Bangladesh, and the countries of Africa, like Mozambique,

Table 1   *Average annual income per person (and of richest 20 per cent and poorest 20 per cent) (measured in international dollars) and per cent in poverty*

	Real GDP per person (PPP $) (1988)	Richest 20%	Poorest 20%	Per cent population below poverty line
US	19,850	41,565	4,662	(13)
Canada	17,680	35,454	5,027	(15)
Sweden	14,940	27,419	5,944	—
Germany	14,620	28,200	4,943	(10)
Hong Kong	14,010	32,934	3,783	—
Japan	13,650	25,618	5,944	—
France	13,590	27,586	4,271	(16)
UK	13,060	25,806	3,789	(18)
Italy	13,000	26,780	4,441	(15)
Spain	8,250	16,603	2,858	(19)
Ireland	7,020	—	2,817	(19)
Hungary	5,920	9,599	3,225	—
Korea	5,680	—	1,893	16
Venezuela	5,650	14,308	1,329	—
Mexico	5,320	16,300	1,360	—
Malaysia	5,070	12,953	1,154	27
Yugoslavia	4,860	10,407	1,482	—
Brazil	4,620	14,469	554	—
Syria	4,460	—	1,301	—
Argentina	4,360	—	1,553	—
WORLD	4,340	—	—	—
Costa Rica	4,320	11,789	714	—
Poland	4,190	7,366	2,029	—
Colombia	3,810	10,100	762	—
Panama	3,790	10,500	715	25
Thailand	3,280	10,600	1,050	30
Peru	3,080	7,200	616	—
Jamaica	2,630	6,472	700	80
Botswana	2,510	7,420	314	51
Guatemala	2,430	6,682	637	71
Morocco	2,380	4,692	1,168	37
Philippines	2,170	5,141	588	58
Sri Lanka	2,120	5,954	510	—
Egypt	1,930	4,900	819	23
Indonesia	1,820	3,763	803	39
Pakistan	1,790	4,078	695	30
Cote d'Ivoire	1,430	3,768	355	28
Kenya	1,010	—	191	44
Ghana	970	2,159	315	44
India	870	1,802	353	48
Bangladesh	720	1,336	373	86

Source: United Nations Development Programme (1991), Tables 17 and 38. United Nations Development Programme (1992), Technical Note Table 2.3. EUROSTAT (1990a). Ross, D. P., and Shillington, R. (1989). Sarpellon, G. (1992).

Somalia, Mali and Ethiopia. Thus, GNP per person was US $12,510 for the industrialised countries but only US $230 for the "least developed countries" in 1988 (as defined by the UN General Assembly). This suggests a ratio of 54:1.

However, comparisons expressed by using exchange rates can be very misleading. Cash economies are variable in their scope, and exchange rates can be unhelpful in measuring the value of goods and services that are available in different countries. The UN International Comparison Project (ICP) has sought to develop comparable international measures of real GDP using purchasing power parities (PPP) instead of exchange rates as conversion factors. These are expressed in international dollars. The consequence of this revaluation has been to diminish the gap in income between rich and poor countries. Thus the income of the industrialised countries was revalued at PPP $14,350 and of the least developed countries at PPP $720 per person in 1988. This produces a ratio of 20:1—notably smaller than the exchange rate ratio. The measured difference between rich and poor countries is still very great but not as extreme as initially suggested.

However, this is only a modest start in improving comparability. The value of home production, unpaid family and community services, freely available natural resources, and location as well as environment, are among the complex issues requiring investigation and evaluation. Oversimplification of measurement can mislead those who produce policies as well as those whose job it is to interpret and explain world patterns. On the other hand, technical sophistication is used by elites to establish their ascendancy in debates about the interpretation of, as well as action upon, the "facts." Some of the documentary work of the United Nations Development Programme in the early 1990s is setting a constructive example. At least the efforts to establish a common basis of international information holds out the prospect of uncovering well-documented examples of advantages which poor countries hold over their rich counterparts.

THIRD WORLD DESTITUTION

Many millions in the Third World are living at standards which can be described only as those of utter destitution. This can be easily seen by comparing countries at the head and foot of Table 1. In 1988 the United States had an income per person approximately 28 times that of Bangladesh. Even the poorest 20 per cent of the United States population had an income per person 6 times higher than the Bangladesh average.

Bangladesh is a useful starting example, with 116 million population. Its GDP per person corresponds with the average for all 43 "least developed countries." As many as 99 millions in that country, or 86 per cent, are estimated to live in poverty. Food intakes, as measured by calories, has fallen on average from 91 per cent of estimated requirements in 1965 to 83 per cent in 1988, while the same indicator rose during these years for all industrial countries from 124 per cent to 132 per cent. GNP per person also fell steadily (at an average annual rate of 0.3 per cent) from 1965 to 1980 and picked up between 1980 and 1987 (at an annual average rate of 0.8 per cent), but average real earnings per employee declined at a rate of 3 per cent each year during the 1970s and have gone on declining at roughly the same rate during the 1980s. There are estimated to be 13 million malnourished children and 63 million people lacking access to health services as well as 108 million lacking access to sanitation.

There are countries with fewer resources even than Bangladesh. In 1988 16 were listed in the UN Development Programme with fewer resources per person. For many of the poor countries there are no reliable measures of the distribution of income or even of their aggregate resources. And this problem applies particularly to countries in turmoil as a consequence of military occupation, radical change of government, civil war and famine, or a mixture of these events. In the early 1990s the breakup of Yugoslavia, the desperate loss of life in Somalia, the instability created by the warring factions in Afghanistan, the transformation of the Soviet Union into 15 republics, and the plight of the Kurds and the Shi-ite Moslems in Iraq following the Gulf War provide examples of rapid impoverishment of many millions of people. Such dramatic events are often ignored in constructing theories of poverty. Yet they are symptomatic of the swings of fortune which can stabilise in forms of long-lasting oppression or dependency (reminiscent, say, of colonialism and feudalism). They also illustrate again how powerful are the structural forces lurking even in the most orderly of societies which perpetuate extreme poverty and inequalities.

Similarly, the collapse of previously well-regulated cities with the onset of riots, or the continuing abrasive effects of conflict between minorities, as in Northern Ireland, or even the rapid growth of homelessness and unemployment, are also symptomatic of a sudden rise in the percentage of the population found to experience poverty, and have to be incorporated into general theories of trends. Again, local or regional turbulence of this kind tends to be discounted in country-wide explanations of poverty. To seek reasons can be instructive. Theories which depend primarily on long-term biological, psychological or sub-cultural dispositions of individuals . . . cannot accommodate sea-changes in the pattern of material living standards of a population.

Table 1 is intended to illustrate two other features of global living standards. The second and third columns show the incomes, for one of the years between 1979 and 1989, of rich and poor at either end of the spectrum in each country. Each population is divided into fifths. A fifth is of course a substantial section of any population. In the United States it means 50 millions, Japan 25m., the UK, France and Italy between 11 and 12m., Germany 16m., Hungary 2m., Mexico 17m., Poland 8m., Brazil 30m., Thailand 11m., Malaysia 4m., Morocco 5m., the Philippines 12m., Indonesia 36m., India 180m., and Bangladesh 23m. The difference between the richest fifth and the poorest fifth is considerable in all countries. But the poor in the rich countries share living standards with considerable sections of the populations of the poorest countries. Fifty million people in the United States have little more income than the world's average and less in fact than large sections of the populations of countries like Sri Lanka, the Philippines, Morocco and Egypt. The same applies to other countries of the OECD.

Similar paradoxes apply to measures of poverty, although, because they are less comprehensive or consistent, they cannot be demonstrated quite so categorically. In the fourth column of Table 1 measures of the extent of poverty in middle-income and poor countries are reproduced. So far as possible these are measures of income below which a minimum nutritionally adequate diet plus essential non-food requirements are not affordable.

I have put corresponding figures for the richer countries in brackets, not because they are less reliable, but to warn that they often seem to depend in practice on a more generous interpretation of subsistence and hence budgetary need. The United States measure, for example, represents a long tradition of estimating the costs of meeting minimum dietary needs, but which accepts that to cover these costs the measure has to allow for non-food costs in nearly the same proportion as found in practice to be allocated in low-income budgets. The point is not inconsequential, and might be applied to Third World measures.

The figures given for the EC countries are based on a poverty line of half average disposable household expenditure. Although that is a relative measure, a number of commentators call attention to its correspondence with subsistence standards constructed in particular countries. . . .

Despite the reservations which have to be made about the comparability of measures of poverty all the international agencies agree that poverty is less prevalent in industrial countries. For example, some 1.4 billion of the world's 5.3 billion people live in poverty. Other estimates suggest that including those living "along the subsistence margin" with only minimal necessities increases the number of poor to nearly two billion.

About 1.2 billion of the total of 1.4 billion are in the developing countries, but 200 millions are in the industrial countries, including about 30 millions in the United States and 100 millions in the former USSR and Eastern Europe.

DUAL POLICY CONTROL

Since the rich countries possess the greatest influence over the world's economy and, through their connections with international organizations and multinational companies, over the global distribution of resources, they hold the key to the changes taking place in the distribution of incomes *within* as well as *between* countries and the percentage of each population found to be in poverty. In general, their advantage has not changed in recent decades, despite development and financial aid programmes drawn up according to prevailing anti-poverty and development theory and despite the adoption of what are conceived to be noble objectives on the part of the international organisations.

On certain criteria inequalities have widened and material and social deprivation worsened. Thus, GNP per person grew on average in industrial countries between 1965 and 1989 by 2.4 per cent each year but remained static (or more strictly grew by a tiny 0.1 per cent) in least developed countries. And within some at least of the richest countries inequalities have widened and poverty increased within their own territories. Yet they are powerful beyond as well as within their own boundaries. Put very simply, they direct the international organisations controlling distribution and redistribution between countries. And they also largely, if decreasingly, control distribution and redistribution of resources within their own territories. This can be characterised as "dual policy control." Explanations of poverty in the world must therefore deal centrally with this duality—part national, part international.

POVERTY AND INEQUALITY IN RICH COUNTRIES

Accordingly, Table 2 concentrates attention on two countries: the richest country in the world and one which is a representative example of industrial and economic powers of the second rank. Statistical information about trends, inequality and poverty for these two countries is comparatively full. The most striking fact about the United States and the United Kingdom is the sharp increase in inequality in both. My thesis is that rapidly increasing access to international markets, combined with increasing control of the domestic labour market has led to the depression of the incomes of the poor at the same time as the enlargement of the incomes of the rich.

For example, there have been a number of reports in the United States press about the increasing wealth of the rich in the 1980s. The trend applies to some other industrialised countries and is the most urgent and intractable social problem which the nations of the world need to confront. Between 1979 and 1989, as Table 2 shows, the share of "adjusted family income" after tax of the richest 20 per cent of households in the United States increased from 39.0 per cent to 42.1 per cent. In dollars the average income was increased (at 1989 values) from 33,883 to 40,811 per person, or by 6,928 dollars (20.4 per cent).

In the same 10 years the share of total income after tax of the richest 20 per cent in the United Kingdom increased from 36 per cent to 42 per cent. Table 2 brings out the fact that during the 1980s average annual disposable income of this richest group per person increased by as much as £5,304, or 40 per cent. This is one measure of Mrs. Thatcher's collected works. It contradicts all the presuppositions of "trickle-down" and certainly represents the biggest shift in resources from poor to rich of the twentieth century.

In both the United States and the United Kingdom the after-tax income of the richest 1 per cent increased even more dramatically, during the 1980s, by three-fifths and by three-quarters respectively. Although polarisation in these two countries has been exceptional, the trend has also been reported for other industrial countries. What also has to be better recognised is the shift of capital assets to the richest groups in the population. The increase in the real value of wealth-holdings has been an important source of enhanced power for the very rich, in addition to their higher real incomes, despite little apparent change in the percentage distribution of marketable wealth.

In the United States the statistical improvement in the fortunes of the very rich has provoked discussion. Among the possible factors listed as causing that improvement: entrepreneurial initiative following tax cuts; greater candour on the part of those whose taxes have been reduced in reporting their real incomes; relatively faster salary-increases for highly educated workers, especially those with computer skills; the rise of two-earner households; and the growing importance of income from wealth—capital gains, dividends and interest.

These "explanations" are superficial, because either they describe small contributory elements of the story only or they attach excessive importance to the characteristics and motivations of individuals and small groups. In both the US and the UK scientific explanation of changes in structural inequality remains at a primitive and grossly underresourced state. Too few connections are made with the structural forces operating at national and international level.

The trend in the fortunes of the rich has to be linked firmly with trends in poverty and with the restructuring of the world's economy. It is no accident that the "underclass" has fared badly while the "overclass" has been enriched. Both developments have common sources. Between 1979 and 1989, as Table 2 also shows, the share of "adjusted family income" going to the poorest 20 per cent of households in the United States fell from 6.4 per cent to 5.6 per cent and real average income (at 1989 values) from 5,536 to 5,420 dollars (representing a percentage fall of 2.1). There was an even sharper decline for families with children. . . .

Table 2   *Trends in income in real terms of richest and poorest 20 per cent in the US and the UK (standardised for household size and composition) 1979–1989*

Country	Share of total disposable income			
	1979	1989	Change in percentage share	Ratio richest/ poorest
United States				
Richest 20%	39.0	42.1	+3.1	7.5
Poorest 20%	6.4	5.6	−0.8	
United Kingdom				
Richest 20%	36	42	+8	5.2
Poorest 20%	9	8	−1	

	Average annual disposable income per person (in 1989 dollars/pounds)			
			Increase or decrease	Per cent
United States	$	$		
Richest 20%	33,883	40,811	+6,928	+20.4
Poorest 20%	5,536	5,420	−116	−2.1
United Kingdom	£	£	£	Per cent
Richest 20%	13,156	18,460	+5,304	+40.3
Poorest 20%	4,212	4,212	0	0
(Poorest 10%)	3,640	3,432	−208	−5.7

Sources:

United States: Committee on Ways and Means, US House of Representatives (1992), pp. 1356, 1379 and 1383.

United Kingdom: Central Statistical Office, *Social Trends* 22, 1992 edition, London, HMSO, Table 5.19 (equivalised disposable income). Written answers to Parliamentary Questions, Hansard 16 July 1992. EUROSTAT, (1990a). Room (1990).

Organisations like the National Commission to Prevent Infant Mortality had recommended urgent action to deal with the tragically high levels of infant mortality, and a report on behalf of UNICEF had concluded that a quite modest package of new policies could in fact transform the situation of many children in poverty in the United States. There is little doubt about the increase in extent and severity of poverty in a decade. In 1990 over 30 millions in the US, or about 13 per cent, were reported to live below the poverty line.

In the same years the share of total after-tax income of the poorest 20 per cent in the United Kingdom also fell, from 9 per cent to 8 per cent even when incomes are rearranged to take account of family size and composition in a formula approved by the Government. As the lower part of Table 2 also shows, there was no gain at all in their disposable income, and in fact there was a fall in the income of the poorest 10 per cent. These figures merely confirmed the calculations made independently 18 months earlier. The statistics issued from the DSS have been greatly delayed and selective in coverage, and measurement. One report of a substantial rise in lower levels of income turned out to be an error.

In the United Kingdom the polarisation of incomes has taken a variety of forms: people sleeping rough and beggars on the streets; repossessions of homes; imprisonment of larger numbers for debt; electricity disconnections; the reappearance of sweatshops and casual labour, including instances of illegal child labour; a rise in the number of accidents and deaths at work; the loss of employment rights and of different forms of work security; the deterioration of public housing and inner city areas; a sharp increase in theft and crimes of violence; the growth of forms of multiple deprivation; the destruction of public administration and service; and the deepening as well as the growth of mass poverty. As argued in this book, *relative deprivation* in its material and social forms is the key idea in developing a measure and a theory of poverty, and these are the kind of outcomes which can be explained a lot better by applying that idea consistently. And it is the selection of a level of resources which ordinarily marks a threshold of "relative deprivation" which gives meaning and coherence to a scientific theory of poverty. . . .

Ill-health, disability, and premature death are also outcomes of inadequate resources underlying material and social deprivation. Poverty kills. The connection must not be shirked. In several countries diverging incomes have lately been shown to match diverging patterns of mortality.

POLICIES WHICH DEEPEN AND LEGITIMATE POVERTY

The emerging patterns of poverty and wealth in the United States and Britain are deeply engrained, and are being reinforced or modified all the time by the policies which are dominant in those two countries. The policies are national, city-wide and international. They reflect prevailing ideologies and theories about poverty and therefore help to explain the nature and extent of the phenomenon.

At the national level the Los Angeles riots of 1992 provide a vivid example. What effort was made in the following days and weeks to identify the deeper causes of the riots? The debate moved towards extremes. On the one hand, many commentators laughed the White House reaction out of court. This was to impugn the welfare and urban policies of previous Democratic presidencies, which were supposed to have debilitated American communities and families. According to the leader writers of the *New York Times,* for example, any examination of the evidence showed that the War on Poverty of the 1960s had, on the contrary, helped to reduce the extent and severity of poverty and had helped to diminish unrest and forestall further riots.

> America's cities need help. So far, President Bush offers them gratuitous insult. . . . Instead of blaming poor people and the cities that try to help them, Mr. Bush might try finding compassionate solutions. . . . The poor, sick and homeless who roam city streets are not the citizens or the products simply of New York or Los Angeles or Detroit or Chicago. They are America's poor, sick and homeless. America has forgotten its collective responsibility to them during the Reagan-Bush years (*New York Times,* May 1992).

On the other hand, free market economists and many Republicans insisted that more disciplined budgetary controls had to be introduced by way of cuts in public and especially welfare expenditure rather than increases in taxation for the better-off. They saw welfare not as a sickly child in need of better nourishment but as a scrounger upon the taxpayer whose easy access to public funds must be stopped for his and the country's good. These commentators have powerful support. After all, in a speech in Michigan in 1991 which attracted enormous publicity President Bush had said that "programs designed to insure racial harmony generated animosity" and "programs intended to help people out of poverty invited dependency." Such remarks, which have been repeated frequently in the 1980s and early 1990s in much of Europe and especially in the United States, illustrate deep-rooted and wrong-headed political ideology, and also illustrate the absence of scientific information and advice.

QUESTIONS

1. How does poverty in the third world differ from poverty in the developed nations? Refer to the concept of relative deprivation in your answer.
2. Name five of the poorest nations in the world and try to identify some of the structure reasons for the high levels of poverty there.

THE STRUCTURE OF WORK AND THE ECONOMIC PYRAMID

Cynthia Fuchs Epstein

Cynthia Epstein is among the sociologists who have conducted pioneering research on the causes and consequences of gender inequality in the United States and other Western societies. A feminist of long standing, Epstein never allows her ideological positions to interfere with her empirical and theoretical arguments. She invariably seeks the origins of inequality in structural rather than social-psychological forces. Her research on women lawyers and their struggles within male-dominated law firms, for example, has convinced her that there is nothing inherent or "natural" in women's personalities or backgrounds that explains the difficulties they experience in achieving the same status and power as their male colleagues. Rather, she finds patterns of gender discrimination in the structure of work organizations that are independent of any attributes of women themselves.

Epstein does not deny that socialization of male and female children creates differences in their aspirations and in their behavior, but she denies that child socialization explains gender inequality to the extent that commonsense explanations suggest. Even after gender socialization, Epstein argues, when given the chance to succeed in the workplace women will do very well. In consequence, she claims that the seemingly natural differences cited as explanations for gender inequality are "deceptive distinctions": They serve to mask the ways in which social institutions actually channel the achievement of women and men and produce inequalities.

As women have increasingly joined the paid labor force in modern Western societies, scholars interested in issues of gender distinctions and inequality have begun to devote much attention to this phenomenon. Most have focused on the current American context, but a body of knowledge is developing about women's activity in the work force historically as well as across geographic boundaries.

The extent to which the workplace is commonly segregated by sex is striking. In some places the segregation is physical, with men and women separated by buildings or walls within buildings. Sometimes this merely reflects the sex typing of the jobs they do. For example, women performing "women's work" in the textile industry usually work only with other women (under male supervision), and male factory workers working at "men's jobs" in steel plants work in an all-male environment.

Often, however, men and women often are separated not by walls but, as we have seen, by social classifications that define some jobs as male and others as female even though the two sexes occupy much the same physical space. So when male managers work in the same offices with female secretaries, segregation exists in symbolic form. In other cases, men and women may do the same or essentially similar jobs (as janitors and cleaning personnel, for example), but men are assigned one job title and women another. Sex segregation in the workplace also reflects the differential status of men and women, since women's jobs tend to be subordinate to men's and typically offer less prestige and less pay.

Numerous theories have attempted to "explain" the sexual division of labor. When put to the test, some have proven inadequate or questionable in the face of evidence to the contrary, but others have proven to be more reasonable or powerful in explaining the phenomenon.

The explanations generally correspond to cultural perspectives about men's and women's nature. Sociobiologists, as we saw earlier, regard the processes of sex segregation in the work force as a result of "natural" forces stemming from the physiological and psychic characteristics of each sex. They assume a functional relationship between traits they regard as inherited and the gender characteristics of jobs, such as men's aggressiveness and their occupation as "big ticket" salesmen, and women's nurturance and their employment as nurses. But most social scientists offer frameworks that do not rest on a biological model. The major explanations are based on sex-role socialization, human capital, and social structural theories. These explanations are not necessarily mutually exclusive, although some proponents regard them as such.

SOCIALIZATION

The theory of socialization into sex roles focuses on the process by which the sexes assume different personality characteristics, skills, and preferences. This perspective suggests that cultural views of the proper attitudes and behavior for each sex are communicated to boys and girls through the messages of their parents, the images provided by the media, and the communications of teachers and friends; these messages are then internalized, with consequences for adult life. Socialization contributes to sex segregation by creating in males and females specific orientations, preferences, and competencies for occupations that have been defined as sex-appropriate, while leaving men and women disinclined toward or ignorant of opportunities to pursue other occupations. Thus, socialization is often considered to limit the kinds of occupationally relevant training women acquire and to account for women's and men's choices among kinds of work.

Socialization is usually described as beginning in the cradle, where, depending upon their sex, infants receive different treatment and messages about who they are and what they will become. They are dressed in clothing that provides cues, such as color, so that others will be able to identify their sex readily. Given this information, those who attend the child usually act according to a stereotyped view of the infant boy's or girl's nature—for example, demonstrating more rough-and-tumble play with boys than with girls (Maccoby and Jacklin, 1974). Observers' assessments of a child's behavior have been found to vary according to whether they are told they are watching a female or male baby (Will et al., 1974; Condry and Condry, 1976). The attitudes regarding appropriate sex-role behavior that are expressed toward the infant extend through childhood and are internalized by the developing males and females. Researchers in the 1950s, for example, noted how similar behavior of girls and boys was differently interpreted and reinforced by middle-class fathers, a relatively equalitarian group. The findings of a study of the fathers of fifty-six children, which was conducted by Aberle and Naegele (1968), reflected the cultural viewpoints of the times. Of those who admitted that they knew that some boys were "holy terrors in their play groups," none expressed any concern that their sons might be bullies. But some of those who proudly guessed that their boys were "a bit of a devil" were troubled by their "bossy" daughters. Socialization is seen as instilling compliance in girls, keeping them closer to home, giving less importance to their education, and orienting them to marriage and motherhood (Komarovsky, 1953).

During the 1960s and 1970s, hundreds of papers published in books and scientific journals reported research that showed the link between cultural messages and practices, such as the depiction of girls and women in picture books (Nilsen, 1977) and in advertising (Goffman, 1976), and their later assumption of roles as housewives and mothers and their choice of "female" occupational roles as teachers and nurses.

Studies indicate that parents hold higher expectations for the adult futures of their sons than their daughters (Maccoby and Jacklin, 1974; Hoffman, 1977; Marini, 1978), and this attitude is believed to be related to men's greater achievement as measured by promotions, honors, and other distinctions. Parents' expectations that their sons will perform better in mathematics than their daughters (Fennema and Sherman, 1977; see Marini and Brinton, 1984 for an extensive review) supposedly account for boys' superior performance in mathematics beyond grade nine.

By the time the child reaches middle to late adolescence, occupational aspirations are almost as sex typed as the workplace itself. Young women aspire to a smaller number of occupations than men (Gottfredson, 1978; Marini and Brinton, 1984), presumably because of the socialization experience.

The focus on early socialization in the belief that it results in distinctive and enduring traits and attitudes in girls and boys has been challenged in many studies (see Reskin and Hartmann, 1986, for a review), including my own (Epstein, 1973a, 1976c). Even in 1970, when I was convinced of the impact of socialization in determining women's sex-typical choices, I wondered if they actually became the people the stereotypes predicted. In *Woman's Place* (1970a) I asked whether the women these girls become, "once attuned to the opinions of parents and family," are actually sensitized to the opinions and preferences of others (other-directed in the sense described by David Riesman in 1953). A speculation current at the time held that women had a propensity to be more people-oriented than object-oriented and that their empathic qualities led many women into social welfare, nursing, and similar work (see Marini and Brinton, 1984, for a review). It seemed to me, however, that "whether this is an innate or an indoctrinated propensity, indeed whether or not women are in fact more compassionate, empathetic, and more interested in people than are men, is yet to be scientifically demonstrated. But there is no doubt that women are thought to be so and this belief has manifold consequences for society's allocation of womanpower" (Epstein, 1970a: 22). I might have added that this also had consequences for social researchers' belief in personality differences between men and women, but bias in methodology was not yet on the agenda.

Knowledge of the relationship between so-called socializing experiences and later behavior is still very limited. Some social researchers have exhibited remarkable selectivity among the indicators they use to predict or explain later behavior. How much is a girl's occupational choice affected by her being given a dress or overalls to wear or a doll or truck to play with?

Reskin and Hartmann (1986) point out in their review of factors leading to sex segregation in the workplace that there is no direct evidence linking sex-role socialization and occupational outcomes. They speculate that the differential socialization of the sexes probably contributes to occupational segregation to some degree, through the formation of both sex-typed preferences in workers and workers' preferences for a particular gender among employers, but there is no established line of causality. They do presume, as do the social scientists Brim, Riley, Kohn, and Schooler, that socialization is a lifelong process, continuing long after childhood and adolescence. Some adult women who have had traditional sex-role socialization have nevertheless gone into nontraditional occupations such as blue-collar crafts (Walshok, 1981) or law (Epstein, 1981b), and there have been successful interventions to reorient or resocialize girls and boys through the use of films and special programs (Atkin, 1975; Flerx et al., 1976; Davidson et al., 1979).

The impact of socialization probably depends not on any single act or set of acts or influences but on their consistency and the absence of other socializing experiences, particularly later in the life cycle. It also depends on the way society defines the links between early experiences and later social roles. For example, boys who become doctors are disproportionately apt to have had fathers who were doctors. An expected assumption of the father's mantle and the father's socializing behavior as a role model are presumed to orient the boy toward medicine, intellectual capacity permitting. This may be true only in a society that permits independent choice or espouses it as a credo. In most societies of the past and in many today, men and women follow in the footsteps of their parents not only because their parents are role models but also because custom, tradition, and social pressure from parents and community make other choices difficult if not impossible.

The need for constant enforcement of social controls on the behavior of men and women through formal and informal punishments and rewards indicates that socialization has only limited impact on the creation of "natural" behavior for each sex. When social controls are relaxed, stereotypes may be undermined by people's expression of their individual interests and talents.

HUMAN CAPITAL THEORY

Neoclassical economic theory is at the heart of the human capital model, which ascribes occupational segregation and women's assignment to poorer jobs to rational economic choices. The theory stipulates that economic behavior is governed by the free choices of individuals attempting to maximize their utility. According to this view, people also marry to increase their utility, and the resulting division of roles between breadwinner and homemaker is based on their assessment of the benefits likely to accrue to the family from this arrangement.

Mincer and Polachek (1974, 1978) and Polachek (1976, 1978, 1979, 1981a, 1981b) have argued that women's actual or expected family obligations dictate a choice of predominantly female occupations. Following human capital theory, they believe that people invest in training or choose certain occupations with the goal of maximizing their lifetime earnings. Because most women expect to leave work when they become mothers, they do not invest in the specialized training that would lead to careers but instead choose occupations that do not penalize intermittent employment, that require only skills that do not depreciate, and that offer relatively high starting wages (although small promise of advancement). As a result of these choices, women are concentrated in predominantly female occupations that characteristically do not reward job experience.

It follows that even those wives who work full time would prefer jobs that do not require overtime or unanticipated work effort, or travel or geographic mobility, and that permit flexibility and time off in domestic emergencies. According to Reskin and Hartmann (1986), these conditions are "all hypothetical characteristics of *some* predominantly female occupations," although they are not actually the case for many others.

The National Academy of Sciences committee that was formed to evaluate the causes of sex segregation in the United States found that human capital theory failed to explain sex segregation in the workplace. Citing theoretical objections, the committee's report asserted that if it were a matter of women seeking jobs requiring less training, there would be no reason to expect them to cluster particularly in female-dominated jobs because many male-dominated jobs also require little skill or training (Blau and Jusenius, 1976) and they pay better than women's jobs. Further, it noted that it was difficult to establish the direction of causation between the patterns of intermittency exhibited by women and their choice of work that is often characterized by little wage growth (Marini and Brinton, 1984). The question is—do women choose such occupations or simply accept what is offered? Posed against a vision of choice and preference is the fact of social constraint.

The concept of human capital has generated considerable research, little of it easily assessed. Economists using the same data often disagree about their interpretation and develop simulation models built on different assumptions. Mincer and Polachek (1974, 1978) attributed the observed relationship of women's work experience, home time, and wages to the decline of their skills while out of the labor force. But the human capital approach has been criticized for failing to take into account the ways in which the attributes of jobs, rather than family responsibilities, affect women's behavior. Low wages and discrimination can affect the choices women or men make in gaining work experience. And both women and men may quit because of undesirable job features (such as distance from home or an oppressive supervisory structure), even if doing so may limit opportunities for promotion (Reskin and Hartmann, 1986).

The human capital approach depends on determining women's assessment of their earning power. They believe that women's expectations that they will interrupt labor-force participation to have children affect their decisions about education, training, and occupation, such as the choice to maximize starting salaries by choosing female-dominated occupations, which hypothetically start at higher wage levels but yield lower long-run returns for experience than do predominately male occupations, which hypothetically offer less to start because they provide on-the-job training and advancement opportunity (Zellner, 1975). In their overview, Reskin and Hartmann (1986) point out that theorists in this tradition make assumptions about women's reasoning without data on the decision-making process. Furthermore, when behavior is subject to such strong structural and cultural constraints as the choice of women's work, there is less reason to expect a theory that assumes economic optimization to hold.

SOCIAL STRUCTURAL ANALYSIS

The assessment of the National Academy of Sciences committee was that job tracks for both men and women are strongly influenced by the opportunities available. Women's opportunities are restricted because of barriers that limit their access to occupations customarily dominated by men. Such barriers include entrance requirements for training and apprenticeship programs. Other barriers are created by employer discrimination, which may stem from prejudices held by both employers and workers based on beliefs about female and male workers' characteristics and the "appropriate" gender for work in particular jobs. Women's positive responses to new job opportunities made available when employers have stopped discriminating or have established affirmative action programs have demonstrated the importance of genuine opportunities for job choice and advancement (Reskin and Hartmann, 1986).

The analysis of the division of labor is complex. We will examine further the social structural approach, but first we must see how the study of social mobility in sociology illustrates the way in which various frameworks have illuminated certain issues regarding men's and women's relative social standing in the occupational world.

Mobility in the United States is achieved primarily by occupational placement. For a long time, the study of mobility was essentially the study of men. As was discussed earlier, women's occupations were not regarded as a source of their social standing; rather, it was their husband's or father's occupation that rooted them in the social structure. Certain sophisticated methodological approaches to the study of social mobility have obscured the role of sex status in mobility processes and socioeconomic states. "Women" and "men" as unitary categories are used as variables, for example, but the use of these categories tends to deflect attention from important differences that emanate from other variables, such as education. The availability of measurement tools became the force driving the study of mobility which began in the 1970s, and sex became a variable along with a vast array of others (Tyree and Hodge, 1978).

Students of stratification have explored the relative social standing or occupational prestige of women and men, the achieved and derived sources of female status, and the mobility rates and processes of men and women. Furthermore, women's occupational status has been taken into account by a number of researchers (Rossi et al., 1974; Felson and Knoke, 1974; Ritter and Hargens, 1975; Hiller and Philliber, 1978; Philliber and Hiller, 1978; Nilson, 1976; Jackman and Jackman, 1983) who concluded that the social standing of women was derived partly from their employment and partly from their mental outlook (although they expressed reservations owing to contradictory findings). Peter Rossi and associates (1974; Sampson and Rossi, 1975; Nock and Rossi, 1978) demonstrated that wives' occupational status can raise the social position of the family, showing the importance of looking at women's social position as well as their husbands' occupations in determining the class position of a family.

In her excellent review of the literature on stratification Acker (1980) points out that some surprising findings about social mobility rates and processes of status attainment say something about the measures used to study stratification. For example, the findings of several prominent social scientists (Treiman and Terrell, 1975b; Featherman and Hauser, 1976; McClendon, 1976) that the process of status attainment—that is, the effect of education and family background on socioeconomic level—is the same for men and women and, even more surprisingly, that their mean occupational status is approximately equal seem doubtful and contrary to experience.

Hauser and Featherman (1977), in their sophisticated analysis of comparative mobility, found similarity of occupational rank after removing the effects of sex differences in the probability of labor-force participation and in occupational distribution. Acker notes:

> Thus the destination of women, where they end up in the system of rewards, is very different from that of men even though the distances from fathers' occupation do not differ radically for women and men. It is not surprising that few differences remain when most of the sources of difference have been removed from the analysis. The finding of equal average occupational status is also misleading, for while mean status equality may exist at any one time, this is an artifact of the distribution of people in jobs. (1989: 27–28)

As is evident to most observers, researchers have shown that the highest status levels are dominated by men (Bose, 1973) and, perhaps a little less obvious, that men generally experience a rise in status over the life cycle, whereas most women stay at about the same status level from the beginning to the end of their working lives (Wolf and Rosenfeld, 1978). Featherman and Hauser (1976), Suter and Miller (1973), and Treiman and Terrell (1975b) have found that the income disadvantages suffered by most women are persistent and severe; even when they improve their job status, they do not generally benefit from the kind of rewards men receive as they climb a ladder of success.

Some studies measure social standing by comparing the prestige of occupations, measured by scales composed of ranks assigned to various kinds of work. According to these measures, women's jobs rank comparably with men's jobs. But what do prestige scales measure? They do not seem to be congruent with common perceptions, and although common perceptions are often wrong, the discrepancy leads us to question the anomalous finding. On review, we find that women with prestige scores similar to those of men do not have similar incomes, nor do they have similar authority in the workplace (Wolf and Fligstein, 1979). Bose (1980) has found that housewives in the United States were ranked highly on a scale measuring prestige of occupations. Yet, even more than before, women pejoratively characterize themselves as "only" housewives, and certainly men would consider "housewife" a low-ranking position if they were to hold it. Acker (1980) holds that the housewife's prestige score reflects a generalized respect for women (a middling sort of respect) and that one source of the prestige attributed to other predominantly female occupations is the generalized respect women earn as mothers and wives.

Some studies of occupational prestige consider such matters as job authority (Spaeth, 1979), skill and task complexity (Baron and Bielby, 1980), and variation along a continuum ranking jobs from bad to good (Doeringer and Piore, 1971). But whatever the underlying dimensions of occupational prestige scores, it is clear that they do not accurately reflect sex inequality in the domain of paid work. The commitment to these elaborate measures continues, however, in spite of critiques by such sociologists as Wolf and Fligstein (1979) and Rosenfeld (1978). Furthermore, the underlying model, which focuses on a single status rather than a status-set (the array of statuses a person has), cannot capture the nature of sex inequality. Conceptualization of the status-attainment model is rooted in the human capital theory of neoclassical economics, which assumes an open, fully competitive market where individual characteristics are identified and rewarded according to their societal value. It resembles the structural-functional stratification theory of Davis and Moore (1945) in considering the financial sacrifices people make to obtain education—both the cost of education and the income forgone during the training period—as an investment in future higher earnings. Both models regard positional rank as a product of individual inputs such as talent, skills, and motivation and presuppose a uniform and freely competitive labor market.

A structural analysis that does not focus on individual characteristics of workers has been offered by investigators using a theory of a dual economy and labor market segmentation. Bibb and Form (1977) find merit in a model that differentiates between what they term core and peripheral industrial establishments—a differentiation based on material and organizational resources. Core establishments are large, capital-intensive forms that practice economies of scale and earn relatively high and stable profits. Peripheral establishments have few material organizational resources; they are small, labor intensive, and geographically scattered. Some textile manufacturers, restaurants, and hospitals are in this category. Workers in core establishments earn appreciably higher salaries than those in the periphery. Bibb and Form assert that their model explains three times as much variance in blue-collar earnings as a human capital model. Both sexes are at a disadvantage in peripheral industries, but since women tend to work disproportionately in these industries because of lack of access to core industries, their location explains some of the discrepancies between the sexes in gross earnings. But this model also has its limitations. Beck, Horan, and Tolbert (1980) show that compared to men most women with high levels of schooling and experience suffer more wage discrimination in core than in peripheral forms. This may be due to the sex segregation of work that exists there. Their interpretation of the sector-specific occupational distributions suggests that this type of discrimination results from the concentration of highly schooled females in the professions within the peripheral sector but their disproportionate location in clerical occupations within the core sector (p. 122).

Sociologists have become aware of different forms of sex segregation in the workplace and their consequences for the social standing of men and women. Sex segregation is only one element, however, in new conceptualizations of stratification. Attention is being given to other structural arrangements—economic and organizational characteristics of the workplace, such as occupational sponsorship, job ceilings for women and blacks, the organizational power of unions, and the economic power of the industry (Bibb and Form, 1977), a matter that has consequences for the rank of men as well as women in the stratification system (Villemez, 1977; Treiman and Terrell, 1975b; Wolf and Rosenfeld, 1978; Feuerberg, 1978).

Although much of Marxist theory is devoted to explaining inequality, it fails to account for the subordination of women. The most productive theory on the subject in the Marxist tradition is its view of women as a reserve army of labor in the capitalist economy. Simeral (1978) argues that women have constituted a cyclical reserve, entering the labor force when demand is high and leaving it when demand contracts. She counters those critics who point out that women have never formed a reserve for men's jobs (Milkman, 1976) by claiming that women do not have to substitute directly for men to have an effect on the market and the overall wage rate.

Yet there are problems with attempts to explain female disadvantage solely on the basis of analysis of the processes of capital expansion and capital accumulation. Women's situation in the industrial reserve army is tempered by their unpaid labor in the home and their role in the reproduction of the labor force. Some scholars working within a Marxist perspective consider this by identifying patriarchy as a component of a system that subordinates women. They argue that the two structures, capitalism and patriarchy, are interrelated in complex ways and must be analyzed together in order to understand the position of women. Two currents of thought can be identified among the Marxists. One argues that the material bases of patriarchy are to be found in human reproduction and in sexuality (Firestone, 1972). Male control of both these spheres leads to the subordination of women and is perpetuated because of men's desire to ensure their paternity of their wives' children. Men therefore create a culture (patriarchy) with women universally subjugated even to the interstices of the unconscious (Mitchell, 1971). The other current of thought roots patriarchy in men's objective economic interests, which cut across class interest. Hartmann (1976), for example, argues that capitalism develops out of a preindustrial patriarchal society and preserves patriarchy as part of the system of control. In the process of development male workers gain a privileged position by denying women access to apprenticeships and jobs in male-dominated, unionized fields and by pushing for protective legislation. Thus as the economy develops it does so with a sex-segregated labor force.

Strober (1982) believes that the interests of men in maintaining a system in which women serve them in the home accounts for their resistance to women's access to equal opportunity in the workplace. Although one can agree that it serves any dominant group to keep subordinate those over whom it has power, not all men have done so, and institutions have differed in the extent to which they have insisted on and ensured women's subordination. In some institutions, policies are distinct; in others there may be no policy at all. A good example of this is the American public grade school system, which, as Hansot and Tyack (1988) point out, followed from its inception the norm of coeducation. Institutions at the high school and university level, however, differed considerably more. In Europe and in many countries of the third world, governments have made specific policies segregating both education and occupations. Such policies have not been specified by the U.S. government except in the military, and that is diminishing to some extent. But policymakers in various occupations and workers themselves have made and still make decisions regarding sex integration or exclusion that affect equal opportunity.

REFERENCES

Aberle, David F., and Kaspar Naegele. "Middle-Class Fathers' Occupational Role and Attitudes toward Children." In Bell and Vogel, eds., *A Modern Introduction to the Family,* rev. ed. (New York: Free Press, 1968): 188–198.

Acker, Joan. "Women and Stratification: A Review of Recent Literature." *Contemporary Sociology* 9 (January 1980): 25–39.

Atkin, Charles K. "Effects of Television Advertising on Children: Second Year Experimental Evidence." Manuscript, 1975, cited in Reskin and Hartmann, eds., *Women's Work, Men's Work: Sex Segregation on the Job* (Washington, D.C.: National Academy Press, 1986).

Baron, J. N., and W. T. Bielby. "Workers and Machines: A Missing Link in Current Stratification Research." Paper presented at the Annual Meeting of the American Sociological Association, New York, 1980.

Beck, E. M., Patrick M. Horan, and Charles M. Tolbert II. "Industrial Segmentation and Labor Market Discrimination." *Social Problems* 28 (2) (December 1980): 113–130.

Bibb, Robert, and William H. Form. "The Effects of Industrial, Occupational and Sex Stratification on Wages in Blue Collar Markets." *Social Forces* 55 (4) (1977): 974–996.

Blau, Francine D., and Carol L. Jusenius. "Economists' Approaches to Sex Segregation in the Labor Market: An Appraisal." In Blaxall and Reagan, eds., *Women in the Workplace* (Chicago: University of Chicago Press, 1976): 181–99.

Bose, Christine. *Jobs and Gender: Sex and Occupational Prestige* (Baltimore: Johns Hopkins University, Center for Metropolitan Planning and Research, 1973).

————. "Social Status of the Homemaker." In Berk, ed., *Women and Household Labor* (Beverly Hills: Sage, 1980): 69–87.

Condry, John, and Sandra Condry. "Sex Differences: A Study of the Eye of the Beholder." *Child Development* 47 (1976): 812–819.

Davidson, Kenneth, Ruth Ginsburg, and Herma Kay. *Sex-Based Discrimination: Text, Cases and Materials* (St. Paul, Minn.: West, 1979).

Davis, Kingsley, and Wilbert E. Moore. "Some Principles of Stratification." *American Sociological Review* 10 (April 1945): 242–249.

Doeringer, Peter B., and Michael J. Piore. *Internal Labor Markets and Manpower Analysis* (Lexington, Mass.: D. C. Heath, 1971).

Epstein, Cynthia Fuchs. *Woman's Place: Options and Limits in Professional Careers* (Berkeley: University of California Press, 1970a).

————. "Bringing Women In: Rewards, Punishments and the Structure of Achievement." *Annals of the New York Academy of Sciences* 108 (March 1973a): 62–70.

————. "Sex Roles." In R. K. Merton and R. Nisher, eds., *Social Problems,* 4th ed. (New York: Harcourt Brace Jovanovich, 1976c).

————. *Women in Law* (New York: Basic Books, 1981b).

Featherman, David L., and Robert M. Hauser. "Sexual Inequalities and Socioeconomic Achievement in the United States, 1962–1973." *American Sociological Review* 41(3) (June 1976): 462–483.

Felson, Marcus, and David Knoke. "Social Status and the Married Woman." *Journal of Marriage and the Family* 36(1974): 116–121.

Fennema, Elizabeth, and Julia Sherman. "Sex-Related Differences in Mathematics Achievements, Spatial Visualization and Affective Factors." *American Educational Research Journal* 14 (1977): 51–71.

Feuerberg, Marvin. "Sexual Inequality: A Theoretical and Empirical Exploration." (Ph.D. diss., University of Oregon, 1978, cited in Acker, 1980).

Firestone, Shulamith. *The Dialectic of Sex* (New York: Bantam Books, 1972).

Flerx, Vicki C., Dorothy S. Fidler, and Ronald W. Rogers. "Sex Role Stereotypes: Developmental Aspects and Early Intervention." *Child Development* 47 (1976): 998–1007.

Goffman, Erving. *Gender Advertisements* (London: Macmillan, 1976).

Gottfredson, Linda S. *Race and Class Differences in Occupational Aspirations: Their Development and Consequences for Occupational Segregation.* Center for Social Organization of Schools Report no. 254 (Baltimore: Johns Hopkins University Press, 1978).

Hansot, E., and D. Tyack. "Gender in American Public Schools: Thinking Institutionally." *Signs* 13(4) (Summer 1988).

Hauser, Robert M., and David L. Featherman. *The Process of Stratification: Trends and Analyses* (New York: Academic Press, 1977).

Hiller, D. V., and W. W. Philliber. "Derivation of Status Benefits from Occupational Attainments of Working Wives." *Journal of Marriage and the Family* 40 (1978): 63–69.

Hoffman, S. "Marital Instability and the Economic Status of Women." *Demography* 14 (1977): 67–76.

Jackman, Mary, and Robert Jackman. *Class Awareness in the United States* (Berkeley: University of California Press, 1983).

Komarovsky, Mirra. *Women in the Modern World* (Boston: Little, Brown, 1953; New York: Irvington Books, 1971).

Maccoby, Eleanor E., and Carol N. Jacklin. *The Psychology of Sex Differences* (Stanford, Calif.: Stanford University Press, 1974).

Marini, Margaret Mooney. "Sex Differences in the Determination of Adolescent Aspirations: A Review of Research." *Sex Roles* 4(5) (1978): 723–753.

Marini, Margaret Mooney, and Mary Brinton. "Sex Typing in Occupational Socialization." In Reskin, ed., *Sex Segregation in the Workplace* (Washington, D.C.: National Academy Press, 1984): 192–232.

McClendon, McKee J. "The Occupational Status Attainment Process of Males and Females." *American Sociological Review* 41(1) (1976): 52–64.

Milkman, Ruth. "Women's Work and Economic Crisis—Some Lessons of the Great Depression." *Review of Radical Politics* 8(1) (1976): 73–97.

Mincer, Jacob, and Solomon Polachek. "Family Investments in Human Capital: Earnings of Women." *Journal of Political Economy* 82(pt. 2) (March–April 1974): S76–S108.

———. "Women's Earnings Reexamined." *Journal of Human Resources* 13 (Winter 1978): 118–134.

Mitchell, Juliet. *Psychoanalysis and Feminism.* (New York: Pantheon, 1971).

Nilsen, Alleen Pace. *Sexism and Language* (Urbana, Ill.: National Council of Teachers of English, 1977).

Nilson, Linda Burzotta. "The Social Standing of a Married Woman." *Social Problems* 23 (1976): 582–591.

Nock, Steven L., and Peter H. Rossi. "Ascription versus Achievement in the Attribution of Family Social Status." *American Journal of Sociology* 84 (1978): 565–590.

Philliber, William H., and Dana V. Hiller. "The Implication of a Wife's Occupational Attainment for Husband's Class Identification." *Sociological Quarterly* 19(3) (1978): 450–458.

Polachek, Solomon. "Occupational Segregation: An Alternative Hypothesis." *Journal of Contemporary Business* 5 (Winter 1976): 1–12.

———. "Sex Differences in Education: An Analysis of the Determinants of College Major." *Industrial and Labor Relations Review* 31 (1978): 498–508.

———. "Occupational Segregation among Women: Theory, Evidence and a Prognosis." In Lloyd, Andrews, and Gilroy, eds., *Women in the Labor Market* (New York: Columbia University Press, 1979).

———. "Occupational Self-Selection: A Human Capital Approach to Sex Differences in Occupational Structure." *Review of Economics and Statistics* 63(1) (February 1981a): 60–69.

———. "A Supply Side Approach to Occupational Segregation." Paper presented at the Annual Meeting of the American Sociological Association, Toronto, August 1981b.

Reskin, Barbara F., and Heidi Hartmann. *Women's Work, Men's Work: Sex Segregation in the Job* (Washington, D.C.: National Academy Press, 1986).

Ritter, K. V., and L. L. Hargens. "Occupational Positions and Class Identifications: A Test of the Asymmetry Hypothesis." *American Journal of Sociology* 80 (1975): 934–948.

Rosenfeld, Rachel A. "Women's Intergenerational Occupational Mobility." *American Sociological Review* 43(1) (1978): 36–46.

Rossi, Peter H., William A. Sampson, Christine E. Bose, Guillermina Jasso, and Jeff Passel. "Measuring Household Social Standing." *Social Science Research* 3(3) (1974): 169–190.

Sampson, William A., and Peter H. Rossi. "Race and Family Standing." *American Sociological Review* 40(2) (1975): 201–214.

Simeral, Margaret H. "Women and the Reserve Army of Labor." *Insurgent Sociology* 8(2–3) (1978): 164–179.

Spaeth, J. L. "Vertical Differentiation among Occupations." *American Sociological Review* 44 (October 1979): 746–762.

Strober, Myra. "The M.B.A.: Same Passport to Success for Women and Men?" In Wallace, ed., *Women in the Workplace* (Boston: Auburn House, 1982): 25–44.

Suter, Larry E., and Herman P. Miller. "Income Differences between Men and Career Women." *American Journal of Sociology* 78(4) (1973): 200–212.

Treiman, D. J., and K. Terrell. "Women, Work and Wages: Trends in the Female Occupational Structure since 1940." In Land and Spilerman, eds., *Social Indicator Models* (New York: Russell Sage Foundation, 1975b): 157–200.

Tyree, Andrea, and Robert W. Hodge. "Editorial Foreword: Five Empirical Landmarks." *Social Forces* 56(3) (1978): 761–769.

Villemez, Wayne J. "Male Economic Gain from Female Subordination: A Caveat and Reanalysis." *Social Forces* 56(2) (1977): 626–636.

Walshok, Mary L. *Blue Collar Women* (New York: Doubleday, 1981; Anchor Books, 1983).

Will, Jerrie, Patricia Self, and Nancy Datan. "Maternal Behavior and Sex of Infant." Paper presented at the Annual Meeting of the American Psychological Association.

Wolf, Wendy, and Neil Fligstein. "Sexual Stratification: Differences in Power in the Work Setting." *Social Forces* 58 (1979): 94–107.

Wolf, Wendy, and Rachel Rosenfeld. "Sex Structure of Occupations and Job Mobility." *Social Forces* 56(3) (1978): 823–844.

Zellner, Harriet. "The Determinants of Occupational Segregation." In Cynthia Lloyd, ed., *Sex Discrimination and the Division of Labor* (New York: Columbia University Press, 1975): 125–145.

QUESTIONS

1. Does Cynthia Fuchs Epstein believe that "genes are destiny"? Explain your answer.
2. What are some of the structural features that might help explain patterns of gender discrimination in economic institutions, according to Epstein?

Part IV: Social Institutions

POLITICS AND THE ENGLISH LANGUAGE

George Orwell

George Orwell is best known as the author of a political satire, Animal Farm, *and the anti-utopian novel* 1984. *But this renowned twentieth century English author is also an acclaimed essayist. In many of his essays, Orwell applies a penetrating and critical sociological imagination. His work on poverty and homelessness in England and France (*Down and Out in London and Paris *and* The Road to Wigan Pier*) remain classics in the description of poverty among the homeless and among working people in the period before World War II. Orwell was always interested in the critique of capitalism but disliked any version of Marxism that led to totalitarian ideas like those of Lenin or Stalin. He was also a sworn enemy of fascism and Nazism and a critic of the kind of social thought that led to dictatorship.*

In his essays, Orwell is often concerned with showing how society creates oppressive social conditions. He was particularly interested in the way language is used in governments and organizations of all kinds to mask the realities of actions that would not appear in a positive light if they were described in direct language. His essay "Politics and the English Language" is a timeless classic on this subject. Although it describes wars that are long past, if one listens to the language used today by governments to describe their military actions (e.g., the use of "incursion" instead of "invasion," or "military action" instead of "attack," or "ethnic cleansing" instead of "expulsion" or "genocide") the essay sounds as if it had been written last week. Since so much of what governments, corporations, and other organizations say in their official pronouncements is written in jargon designed for purposes similar to those that Orwell criticizes, this essay is a valuable sociological statement about the origins and uses of such self-serving jargon.

Most people who bother with the matter at all would admit that the English language is in a bad way, but it is generally assumed that we cannot by conscious action do anything about it. Our civilization is decadent and our language—so the argument runs—must inevitably share in the general collapse. It follows that any struggle against the abuse of language is a sentimental archaism, like preferring candles to electric light or hansom cabs to aeroplanes. Underneath this lies the half-conscious belief that language is a natural growth and not an instrument which we shape for our own purposes.

Now, it is clear that the decline of a language must ultimately have political and economic causes: it is not due simply to the bad influence of this or that individual writer. But an effect can become a cause, reinforcing the original cause and producing the same effect in an intensified form, and so on indefinitely. A man may take to drink because he feels himself to be a failure, and then fail all the more completely because he drinks. It is rather the same thing that is happening to the English language. It becomes ugly and inaccurate because our thoughts are foolish, but the slovenliness of our language makes it easier for us to have foolish thoughts. The point is that the process is reversible. Modern English, especially written English, is full of bad habits which spread by imitation and which can be avoided if one is willing to take the necessary trouble. If one gets rid of these habits one can think more clearly, and to think clearly is a necessary first step towards political regeneration: so that the fight against bad English is not frivolous and is not the exclusive concern of professional writers. I will come back to this presently, and I hope that by that time the meaning of what I have said here will have become clearer. Meanwhile, here are five specimens of the English language as it is now habitually written.

These five passages have not been picked out because they are especially bad—I could have quoted far worse if I had chosen—but because they illustrate various of the mental vices from which we now suffer. They are a little below the average, but are fairly representative samples. I number them so that I can refer back to them when necessary:

(1) I am not, indeed, sure whether it is not true to say that the Milton who once seemed not unlike a seventeenth-century Shelley had not become, out of an experience ever more bitter in each year, more alien [sic] to the founder of that Jesuit sect which nothing could induce him to tolerate.

> Professor Harold Laski
> (Essay in *Freedom of Expression*).

(2) Above all, we cannot play ducks and drakes with a native battery of idioms which prescribes such egregious collocations of vocables as the Basic *put up with* for *tolerate* or *put at a loss* for *bewilder.*

> Professor Lancelot Hogben (*Interglossa*).

(3) On the one side we have the free personality: by definition it is not neurotic, for it has neither conflict nor dream. Its desires, such as they are, are transparent, for they are just what institutional approval keeps in the forefront of consciousness; another institutional pattern would alter their number and intensity; there is little in them that is natural, irreducible, or culturally dangerous. But *on the other side,* the social bond itself is nothing but the mutual reflection of these self-secure integrities. Recall the definition of love. Is not this the very picture of a small academic? Where is there a place in this hall of mirrors for either personality or fraternity?

> Essay on psychology in *Politics* (New York).

(4) All the "best people" from the gentlemen's clubs, and all the frantic fascist captains, united in common hatred of Socialism and bestial horror of the rising tide of the mass revolutionary movement, have turned to acts of provocation, to foul incendiarism, to medieval legends of poisoned wells, to legalize their own destruction of proletarian organizations, and rouse the agitated petty-bourgeoisie to chauvinistic fervor on behalf of the fight against the revolutionary way out of the crisis.

> Communist pamphlet.

(5) If a new spirit *is* to be infused into this old country, there is one thorny and contentious reform which must be tackled, and that is the humanization and galvanization of the B.B.C. Timidity here will bespeak canker and atrophy of the soul. The heart of Britain may be sound and of strong beat, for instance, but the British lion's roar at present is like that of Bottom in Shakespeare's *Midsummer Night's Dream*—as gentle as any sucking dove. A virile new Britain cannot continue indefinitely to be traduced in the eyes or rather ears, of the world by the effete languors of Langham Place, brazenly masquerading as "standard English." When the Voice of Britain is heard at nine o'clock, better far and infinitely less ludicrous to hear aitches honestly dropped than the present priggish, inflated, inhibited, school-ma'amish arch braying of blameless bashful mewing maidens!

> Letter in *Tribune.*

Each of these passages has faults of its own, but, quite apart from avoidable ugliness, two qualities are common to all of them. The first is staleness of imagery; the other is lack of precision. The writer either has a meaning and cannot express it, or he inadvertently says something else, or he is almost indifferent as to whether his words mean anything or not. This mixture of vagueness and sheer incompetence is the most marked characteristic of modern English prose, and especially of any kind of political writing. As soon as certain topics are raised, the concrete melts into the abstract and no one seems able to think of turns of speech that are not hackneyed: prose consists less and less of *words* chosen for the sake of their meaning, and more and more of *phrases* tacked together like the sections of a prefabricated hen-house. I list below, with notes and examples, various of the tricks by means of which the work of prose-construction is habitually dodged:

Dying metaphors. A newly invented metaphor assists thought by evoking a visual image, while on the other hand a metaphor which is technically "dead" (e.g. *iron resolution*) has in effect reverted to being an ordinary word and can generally be used without loss of vividness. But in between these two classes there is a huge dump of worn-out metaphors which have lost all evocative power and are merely used because they save people the trouble of inventing phrases for themselves. Examples are: *Ring the changes on, take up the cudgels for, toe the line, ride roughshod over, stand shoulder to shoulder with, play into the hands of, no axe to grind, grist to the mill, fishing in troubled waters, on the order of the day, Achilles' heel, swan song, hotbed.* Many of these are used without knowledge of their meaning (what is a "rift," for instance?), and incompatible metaphors are frequently mixed, a sure sign that the writer is not interested in what he is saying. Some metaphors now current have been twisted out of their original meaning without those who use them even being aware of the fact. For example, *toe the line* is sometimes written *tow the line.* Another example *is the hammer and the anvil,* now always used with the implication that the anvil gets the worst of it. In real life it is always the anvil that breaks the hammer, never the other way about: a writer who stopped to think what he was saying would be aware of this, and would avoid perverting the original phrase.

Operators or verbal false limbs. These save the trouble of picking out appropriate verbs and nouns, and at the same time pad each sentence with extra syllables which give it an appearance of symmetry. Characteristic phrases are *render inoperative, militate against, make contact with, be subjected to, give rise to, give grounds for, have the effect of, play a leading part (role) in, make itself felt, take effect, exhibit a tendency to, serve the purpose of, etc., etc.* The keynote is the elimination of simple verbs. Instead of being a single word, such as *break, stop, spoil, mend, kill,* a verb becomes a *phrase,* made up of a noun or adjective tacked on to some general-purposes verb such as *prove, serve, form, play, render.* In addition, the passive voice is wherever possible used in preference to the active, and noun constructions are used instead of gerunds (*by examination of* instead of *by examining*). The range of verbs is further cut down by means of the *-ize* and *de-* formations, and the banal statements are given an appearance of profundity by means of the *not un-* formation. Simple conjunctions and prepositions are replaced by such phrases as *with respect to, having regard to, the fact that, by dint of, in view of, in the interests of, on the hypothesis that;* and the ends of sentences are saved by anticlimax by such resounding common-places as *greatly to be desired, cannot be left out of account, a development to be expected in the near future, deserving of serious consideration, brought to a satisfactory conclusion,* and so on and so forth.

Pretentious diction. Words like *phenomenon, element, individual* (as noun), *objective, categorical, effective, virtual, basic, primary, promote, constitute, exhibit, exploit, utilize, eliminate, liquidate,* are used to dress up simple statement and give an air of scientific impartiality to biased judgements. Adjectives like *epoch-making, epic, historic, unforgettable, triumphant, age-old, inevitable, inexorable, veritable,* are used to dignify the sordid processes of international politics, while writing that aims at glorifying war usually takes on an archaic color, its characteristic words being: *realm, throne, chariot, mailed fist, trident, sword, shield, buckler, banner, jackboot, clarion.* Foreign words and expressions such as *cul de sac, ancien régime, deus ex machina, mutatis mutandis, status quo, gleichschaltung, weltanschauung,* are used to give an air of culture and elegance. Except for the useful abbreviations *i.e., e.g.,* and *etc.,* there is no real need for any of the hundreds of foreign phrases now current in English. Bad writers, and especially scientific, political and sociological writers, are nearly always haunted by the notion that Latin or Greek words are grander than Saxon ones, and unnecessary words like *expedite, ameliorate, predict, extraneous, deracinated, clandestine, subaqueous* and hundreds of others constantly gain ground from their Anglo-Saxon opposite numbers.[1] The jargon peculiar to Marxist writing (*hyena,*

---

[1]An interesting illustration of this is the way in which the English flower names which were in use till very recently are being ousted by Greek ones, *snapdragon* becoming *antirrhinum, forget-me-not* becoming *myosotis,* etc. It is hard to see any practical reason for this change of fashion: it is probably due to an instinctive turning-away from the more homely word and a vague feeling that the Greek word is scientific.

hangman, cannibal, petty bourgeois, these gentry, lacquery, flunkey, mad dog, White Guard, etc.) consists largely of words and phrases translated from Russian, German or French; but the normal way of coining a new word is to use a Latin or Greek root with the appropriate affix and, where necessary, the size formation. It is often easier to make up words of this kind (*deregionalize, impermissible, extramarital, non-fragmentary* and so forth) than to think up the English words that will cover one's meaning. The result, in general, is an increase in slovenliness and vagueness.

Meaningless words. In certain kinds of writing, particularly in art criticism and literary criticism, it is normal to come across long passages which are almost completely lacking in meaning.[2] Words like *romantic, plastic, values, human, dead, sentimental, natural, vitality,* as used in art criticism, are strictly meaningless, in the sense that they not only do not point to any discoverable object, but are hardly ever expected to do so by the reader. When one critic writes, "The outstanding feature of Mr. X's work is its living quality," while another writes, "The immediately striking thing about Mr. X's work is its peculiar deadness," the reader accepts this as a simple difference of opinion. If words like *black* and *white* were involved, instead of the jargon words *dead* and *living,* he would see at once that language was being used in an improper way. Many political words are similarly abused. The word *Fascism* has now no meaning except in so far as it signifies "something not desirable." The words *democracy, socialism, freedom, patriotic, realistic, justice,* have each of them several different meanings which cannot be reconciled with one another. In the case of a word like *democracy,* not only is there no agreed definition, but the attempt to make one is resisted from all sides. It is almost universally felt that when we call a country democratic we are praising it: consequently the defenders of every kind of régime claim that it is a democracy, and fear that they might have to stop using the word if it were tied down to any one meaning. Words of this kind are often used in a consciously dishonest way. That is, the person who uses them has his own private definition, but allows his hearer to think he means something quite different. Statements like *Marshal Pétain was a true patriot, The Soviet Press is the freest in the world, The Catholic Church is opposed to persecution,* are almost always made with intent to deceive. Other words used in variable meanings, in most cases more or less dishonestly, are: *class, totalitarian, science, progressive, reactionary, bourgeois, equality.*

Now that I have made this catalogue of swindles and perversions, let me give another example of the kind of writing that they lead to. This time it must of its nature be an imaginary one. I am going to translate a passage of good English into modern English of the worst sort. Here is a well-known verse from *Ecclesiastes:*

"I returned and saw under the sun, that the race is not to the swift, nor the battle to the strong, neither yet bread to the wise, nor yet riches to men of understanding, nor yet favour to men of skill; but time and chance happeneth to them all."

Here it is in modern English:

"Objective considerations of contemporary phenomena compels the conclusion that success or failure in competitive activities exhibits no tendency to be commensurate with innate capacity, but that a considerable element of the unpredictable must invariably be taken into account."

This is a parody, but not a very gross one. Exhibit (3), above, for instance, contains several patches of the same kind of English. It will be seen that I have not made a full translation. The beginning and ending of the sentence follow the original meaning fairly closely, but in the middle the concrete illustrations—race, battle, bread—dissolve into the vague phrase "success or failure in competitive activities." This had to be so, because no modern writer of the kind I am discussing—no one capable of using phrases like "objective consideration of contemporary phenomena"—would ever tabulate his thoughts in that precise and detailed way. The whole tendency of modern prose is away from concreteness. Now analyse these two sentences a little more closely. The first contains forty-nine words but only sixty syllables, and all its words are those of everyday life. The second contains thirty-eight words of ninety syllables: eighteen of its words are from Latin roots, and one from Greek. The first sentence contains six vivid images, and only one phrase ("time and chance") that could be called

[2]Example: "Comfort's catholicity of perception and image, strangely Whitmanesque in range, almost the exact opposite in aesthetic compulsion, continues to evoke that trembling atmospheric accumulative hinting at a cruel, an inexorably serene timelessness . . . Wrey Gardiner scores by aiming at simple bull's-eyes with precision. Only they are not so simple, and through this contented sadness runs more than the surface bitter-sweet of resignation." (*Poetry Quarterly.*)

vague. The second contains not a single fresh, arresting phrase, and in spite of its ninety syllables it gives only a shortened version of the meaning contained in the first. Yet without a doubt it is the second kind of sentence that is gaining ground in modern English. I do not want to exaggerate. This kind of writing is not yet universal, and outcrops of simplicity will occur here and there in the worst-written page. Still, if you or I were told to write a few lines on the uncertainty of human fortunes, we should probably come much nearer to my imaginary sentence than to the one from *Ecclesiastes.*

As I have tried to show, modern writing at its worst does not consist in picking out words for the sake of their meaning and inventing images in order to make the meaning clearer. It consists in gumming together long strips of words which have already been set in order by someone else, and making the results presentable by sheer humbug. The attraction of this way of writing is that it is easy. It is easier—even quicker, once you have the habit—to say *In my opinion it is not an unjustifiable assumption that* than to say *I think.* If you use ready-made phrases, you not only don't have to hunt about for words; you also don't have to bother with the rhythms of your sentences, since these phrases are generally so arranged as to be more or less euphonious. When you are composing in a hurry—when you are dictating to a stenographer, for instance, or making a public speech—it is natural to fall into a pretentious, Latinized style. Tags like *a consideration which we should do well to bear in mind* or *a conclusion to which all of us would readily assent* will save many a sentence from coming down with a bump. By using stale metaphors, similes and idioms, you save much mental effort, at the cost of leaving your meaning vague, not only for your reader but for yourself. This is the significance of mixed metaphors. The sole aim of a metaphor is to call up a visual image. When these images clash—as in *The Fascist octopus has sung its swan song, the jackboot is thrown into the melting pot*—it can be taken as certain that the writer is not seeing a mental image of the objects he is naming; in other words he is not really thinking. Look again at the examples I gave at the beginning of this essay. Professor Laski (1) uses five negatives in fifty-three words. One of these is superfluous, making nonsense of the whole passage, and in addition there is the slip *alien* for akin, making further nonsense, and several avoidable pieces of clumsiness which increase the general vagueness. Professor Hogben (2) plays ducks and drakes with a battery which is able to write prescriptions, and, while disapproving of the everyday phrase *put up with,* is unwilling to look *egregious* up in the dictionary and see what it means; (3), if one takes an uncharitable attitude towards it, is simply meaningless: probably one could work out its intended meaning by reading the whole of the article in which it occurs. In (4), the writer knows more or less what he wants to say, but an accumulation of stale phrases chokes him like tea leaves blocking a sink. In (5), words and meaning have almost parted company. People who write in this manner usually have a general emotional meaning—they dislike one thing and want to express solidarity with another—but they are not interested in the detail of what they are saying. A scrupulous writer, in every sentence that he writes, will ask himself at least four questions, thus: What am I trying to say? What words will express it? What image or idiom will make it clearer? Is this image fresh enough to have an effect? And he will probably ask himself two more: Could I put it more shortly? Have I said anything that is avoidably ugly? But you are not obliged to go to all this trouble. You can shirk it by simply throwing your mind open and letting the ready-made phrases come crowding in. They will construct your sentences for you—even think your thoughts for you, to a certain extent—and at need they will perform the important service of partially concealing your meaning even from yourself. It is at this point that the special connection between politics and the debasement of language becomes clear.

In our time it is broadly true that political writing is bad writing. Where it is not true, it will generally be found that the writer is some kind of rebel, expressing his private opinions and not a "party line." Orthodoxy, of whatever color, seems to demand a lifeless, imitative style. The political dialects to be found in pamphlets, leading articles, manifestos, White Papers and the speeches of under-secretaries do, of course, vary from party to party, but they are all alike in that one almost never finds in them a fresh, vivid, home-made turn of speech. When one watches some tired hack on the platform mechanically repeating the familiar phrases—*bestial atrocities, iron heel, bloodstained tyranny, free peoples of the world, stand shoulder to shoulder*—one often has a curious feeling that one is not watching a live human being but some kind of dummy: a feeling which suddenly becomes stronger at moments when the light catches the speaker's spectacles and turns them into blank discs which seem to have no eyes behind them. And this is not altogether fanciful. A speaker who uses that kind of phraseology has gone some distance towards turning himself into a machine. The appropriate noises are coming out of his larynx, but his brain is not involved as it would be if he were choosing his words for himself. If the speech he is making is one that he is accustomed to make over and over again, he may be almost unconscious of what he is saying, as one is when one utters the responses in church. And this reduced state of consciousness, if not indispensable, is at any rate favorable to political conformity.

In our time, political speech and writing are largely the defence of the indefensible. Things like the continuance of British rule in India, the Russian purges and deportations, the dropping of the atom bombs on Japan, can indeed be defended, but only by arguments which are too brutal for most people to face, and which do not square with the professed aims of political parties. Thus political language has to consist largely of euphemism, question-begging and sheer cloudy vagueness. Defenceless villages are bombarded from the air, the inhabitants driven out into the countryside, the cattle machine-gunned, the huts set on fire with incendiary bullets: this is called *pacification.* Millions of peasants are robbed of their farms and sent trudging along the roads with no more than they can carry: this is called *transfer of population* or *rectification of frontiers.* People are imprisoned for years without trial, or shot in the back of the neck or sent to die of scurvy in Arctic lumber camps: this is called *elimination of unreliable elements.* Such phraseology is needed if one wants to name things without calling up mental pictures of them. Consider for instance some comfortable English professor defending Russian totalitarianism. He cannot say outright, "I believe in killing off your opponents when you can get good results by doing so." Probably, therefore, he will say something like this:

"While freely conceding that the Soviet régime exhibits certain features which the humanitarian may be inclined to deplore, we must, I think, agree that a certain curtailment of the right to political opposition is an unavoidable concomitant of transitional periods, and that the rigors which the Russian people have been called upon to undergo have been amply justified in the sphere of concrete achievement."

The inflated style is itself a kind of euphemism. A mass of Latin words falls upon the facts like soft snow, blurring the outlines and covering up all the details. The great enemy of clear language is insincerity. When there is a gap between one's real and one's declared aims, one turns as it were instinctively to long words and exhausted idioms, like a cuttlefish squirting out ink. In our age there is no such thing as "keeping out of politics." All issues are political issues, and politics itself is a mass of lies, evasions, folly, hatred and schizophrenia. When the general atmosphere is bad, language must suffer. I should expect to find—this is a guess which I have not sufficient knowledge to verify—that the German, Russian and Italian languages have all deteriorated in the last ten or fifteen years, as a result of dictatorship.

But if thought corrupts language, language can also corrupt thought. A bad usage can spread by tradition and imitation, even among people who should and do know better. The debased language that I have been discussing is in some ways very convenient. Phrases like *a not unjustifiable assumption, leaves much to be desired, would serve no good purpose, a consideration which we should do well to bear in mind,* are a continuous temptation, a packet of aspirins always at one's elbow. Look back through this essay, and for certain you will find that I have again and again committed the very faults I am protesting against. By this morning's post I have received a pamphlet dealing with conditions in Germany. The author tells me that he "felt impelled" to write it. I open it at random, and here is almost the first sentence that I see: "[The Allies] have an opportunity not only of achieving a radical transformation of Germany's social and political structure in such a way as to avoid a nationalistic reaction in Germany itself, but at the same time of laying the foundations of a co-operative and unified Europe." You see, he "feels impelled" to write—feels, presumably, that he has something new to say—and yet his words, like cavalry horses answering the bugle, group themselves automatically into the familiar dreary pattern. This invasion of one's mind by ready-made phrases (*lay the foundations, achieve a radical transformation*) can only be prevented if one is constantly on guard against them, and every such phrase anaesthetizes a portion of one's brain.

I said earlier that the decadence of our language is probably curable. Those who deny this would argue, if they produced an argument at all, that language merely reflects existing social conditions, and that we cannot influence its development by any direct tinkering with words and constructions. So far as the general tone or spirit of a language goes, this may be true, but it is not true in detail. Silly words and expressions have often disappeared, not through any evolutionary process but owing to the conscious action of a minority. Two recent examples were *explore every avenue* and *leave no stone unturned,* which were killed by the jeers of a few journalists. There is a long list of flyblown metaphors which could similarly be got rid of if enough people would interest themselves in the job; and it should also be possible to laugh the *not un-* formation out of existence,[3] to reduce the amount of Latin and Greek in the average sentence, to drive out foreign phrases and strayed scientific words, and, in general, to make pretentiousness unfashionable. But all these are minor points. The defence of the English language implies more than this, and perhaps it is best to start by saying what it does *not* imply.

To begin with it has nothing to do with archaism, with the salvaging of obsolete words and turns of speech, or with the setting up of a "standard English" which must never be departed from. On the contrary, it is especially concerned with the scrapping of every word or idiom which has outworn its usefulness. It has nothing to do with correct grammar and syntax, which are of no importance so long as one makes one's meaning clear, or with the avoidance of Americanisms, or with having what is called a "good prose style." On the other hand it is not concerned with fake simplicity and the attempt to make written English colloquial. Nor does it even imply in every case preferring the Saxon word to the Latin one, though it does imply using the fewest and shortest words that will cover one's meaning. What is above all needed is to let the meaning choose the word, and not the other way about. In prose, the worst thing one can do with words is to surrender to them. When you think of a concrete object, you think wordlessly, and then, if you want to describe the thing you have been visualizing you probably hunt about till you find the exact words that seem to fit it. When you think of something abstract you are more inclined to use words from the start, and unless you make a conscious effort to prevent it, the existing dialect will come rushing in and do the job for you, at the expense of blurring or even changing your meaning. Probably it is better to put off using words as long as possible and get one's meaning as clear as one can through pictures or sensations. Afterwards one can choose—not simply *accept*—the phrases that will best cover the meaning, and then switch round and decide what impression one's words are likely to make on another person. This last effort of the mind cuts out all stale or mixed images, all prefabricated phrases, needless repetitions, and humbug and vagueness generally. But one can often be in doubt about the effect of a word or a phrase, and one needs rules that one can rely on when instinct fails. I think the following rules will cover most cases:

(i) Never use a metaphor, simile or other figure of speech which you are used to seeing in print.

(ii) Never use a long word where a short one will do.

(iii) If it is possible to cut a word out, always cut it out.

(iv) Never use the passive where you can use the active.

(v) Never use a foreign phrase, a scientific word or a jargon word if you can think of an everyday English equivalent.

(vi) Break any of these rules sooner than say anything outright barbarous.

These rules sound elementary, and so they are, but they demand a deep change of attitude in anyone who has grown used to writing in the style now fashionable. One could keep all of them and still write bad English, but one could not write the kind of stuff that I quoted in those five specimens at the beginning of this article.

I have not here been considering the literary use of language, but merely language as an instrument for expressing and not for concealing or preventing thought. Stuart Chase and others have come near to claiming that all abstract words are meaningless, and have used this as a pretext for advocating a kind of political quietism. Since you don't know what Fascism is, how can you struggle against Fascism? One need not swallow such absurdities as this, but one ought to recognize that the present political chaos is connected with the decay of language, and that one can probably bring about some improvement by starting at the verbal end. If you simplify your English, you are freed from the worst follies of orthodoxy. You cannot speak any of the necessary dialects, and when you make a stupid remark its stupidity will be obvious, even to yourself. Political language—and with variations this is true of all political parties, from Conservatives to Anarchists—is designed to make lies sound truthful and murder respectable, and to give an appearance of solidity to pure wind. One cannot change this all in a moment, but one can at least change one's own habits, and from time to time one can even, if one jeers loudly enough, send some worn-out and useless phrase—some *jackboot, Achilles's heel, hotbed, melting pot, acid test, veritable inferno* or other lump of verbal refuse—into the dustbin where it belongs.

---

[3]One can cure oneself of the *not un-* formation by memorizing this sentence: *A not unblack dog was chasing a not unsmall rabbit across a not ungreen field.*

QUESTIONS

1. Why, according to George Orwell, is there so much euphemism in political speech? Give some examples, either from his essay or from your own experience.

2. How does Orwell believe we should treat the kind of language that so often masks the real intentions or effects of political actions?

THE SOCIAL SOURCES OF DIVISION

Nancy Tatom Ammerman

Nancy Tatom Ammerman is a sociologist of religion who grew up in a deeply religious home and community. A Southern Baptist, she married a Baptist seminarian and has participated in many Baptist congregations in different regions of the United States. She became a sociologist in part to be able to conduct credible research on the subject of religion and religious conflict, which has fascinated her throughout her life.

For her book Baptist Battles, *from which this selection is taken, Ammerman conducted extensive interviews with members of congregations throughout the nation, but especially in the South. She also interviewed many ministers and church leaders. Her field research involved participation in Baptist conventions and gatherings of all kinds. In consequence, her findings are supported by quantitative results, as exemplified in this essay, and deepened by interpretations of the statements made by church leaders and others in personal interviews.*

Ammerman's study is an excellent example of recent research in the sociology of religion. She tries with great success to explain the origins of the divisions within the church and to render each side's viewpoints with clarity and fairness.

Niebuhr hypothesized that those he called the "disinherited" were often the source of religious discontent and of new religious movements. He wrote,

> Whenever Christianity has become the religion of the fortunate and cultured and has grown philosophical, abstract, formal, and ethically harmless in the process, the lower strata of society find themselves religiously expatriated by a faith which neither meets their psychological needs nor sets forth an appealing ethical ideal. In such a situation the right leader finds little difficulty in launching a new movement.[1]

To what extent could such status factors account for the differences between the Convention's right and left wings? Did moderates represent the fortunate, cultured, and formal version of Christianity, while fundamentalists represented the more spontaneous, simple, and unconditioned faith in divine revelation that Troeltsch and Niebuhr saw as more characteristic of people living in need?

We asked our respondents about their financial conditions while growing up and found that there was little theological difference between those who grew up rich and those who grew up poor. There were differences, however, between people who grew up in white collar and professional families and those whose parents were farmers or blue collar workers. Those with higher status parents were twice as likely to be on the left side of the Baptist fence. More than a quarter of them (28 percent) were in the theologically moderate camp, compared to 12 percent of those whose parents farmed and 16 percent of those from blue collar homes. Conversely, those from farming and blue collar families were more likely than those from white collar and professional families to be on the fundamentalist side of the fence. The occupational status, but not the income, of the childhood families from which Baptists came seemed to have some relationship, then, to the beliefs they held and the parties they joined in this fight.

[1]H. R. Niebuhr, *The Social Sources of Denominationalism* (New York: World Publishing, 1929), pp. 31–32.

This suggests that the status differences that may exist between conservative dissidents and the denomination's establishment may be attributed to differences in culture and style of life more than to differences in raw economic privilege. What makes white collar and professional parents different is much more than the amount of money they make or the prestige they may have in the community. White collar parents are much more likely to value independent thinking, creativity, and expressiveness in their children, while blue collar parents often try to teach obedience, routine, and self-control. Those differing values, after all, reflect the differences between working with supervisors and fixed tasks, compared to making one's own schedule and designing one's own work. These differences in up-bringing may be reflected in the theological party differences we see among Southern Baptists.

Their own place in the occupational structure also played a role in where these Baptists stood (see table 1). Again, households in which the husband had a professional job were slightly more likely to be inhabited by moderates than by fundamentalists (27 percent versus 24 percent), and more likely than any other occupational group to contain people left of center. Blue collar and farming households were just the opposite—containing far more fundamentalists than moderates (31 percent versus 7 percent and 34 percent versus 12 percent respectively). Conservative beliefs seemed to have a very strong hold within farming and blue collar households, while those who worked in higher status occupations were somewhat more likely to fall to the left of center and to identify with the moderate party in the denomination. Not only were moderates much more likely to have come from white collar and professional families, they were also more likely to live in such a family as adults. The result was a fairly stark contrast in the occupational composition of the convention's right and left wings. The world of moderates was almost exclusively a white collar and professional world, while fundamentalists were distributed broadly across farming, blue collar, white collar, and professional occupations.

There were also systematic differences in income across these groups (see the middle section of table 1). The higher the respondent's family income, the less likely they were to be fundamentalist. The number of self-identified fundamentalists is relatively constant (except in the highest category), but the number whose *beliefs* are to the right of center falls from 37 percent to 17 percent as people in the lowest income range are compared to those in each higher group. Likewise, the number of people to the left of center *rises* from 2 percent to 35 percent across the same range of income. In the lowest income groups, fundamentalists outnumber moderates almost ten to one, while in the highest income groups, moderates outnumber fundamentalists more than two to one. Those most likely to sympathize with the cause of SBC fundamentalists, then, were those with less income. Those who had made it comfortably into the middle class were still a very conservative lot, but were much more likely than their "disinherited" friends to sympathize with the moderate cause.

The result is a left wing that has a much higher average income than those who are more conservative. Well over one third of moderates reported family incomes over $35,000 in 1984, while fewer than half that many conservatives and fundamentalists were so fortunate. There were enough differences in social standing among Southern Baptists to make it likely that people would be aware of those differences and of the way they corresponded to the theological divisions. Among fundamentalists there was a sense of resentment at the privilege and "snobbery" of the other side. Among moderates there was condescension that varied between snickering and compassion. As Stark and Bainbridge argue, "The conception of who is and who is not 'our kind of people' is endemic in highly stratified groups."[2] In this case, 'our kind of people' had both social class and theological dimensions.

Another indirect measure of status in the Southern Baptist Convention was the size of the church to which one belonged. Bigger churches tended toward the middle- and upper-middle classes, while smaller ones were often thought of as less prestigious. This was even more true among clergy, of course, where the size of a congregation was a way of measuring one's progress up the status ladder in the denomination. It is especially the case that pastors of very large churches (over 1,000 resident members) leaned significantly to the left and were more likely to identify themselves as moderates than pastors of smaller churches. This was all the more striking because this group contains those very few pastors of "super churches" whose responses were quite the opposite. They were few enough in number to be outweighed on average by the moderate sentiments of pastors in other large (but not huge) churches. Without the conservative super-church pastors, this group of clergy might

---

[2]R. Stark and W. S. Bainbridge, *The Future of Religion* (Berkeley: University of California Press, 1985), p. 103.

Table 1   *Percent in Different Theological Parties by Status Factors*

Theological Party	HUSBAND'S OCCUPATIONAL CATEGORY (Laity)				
	Farming	Blue Collar	White Collar	Professional	Average
Self-Identified Moderate	8%	3%	11%	15%	10%
Moderate Conservative	4	4	8	12	8
Conservative	53	62	59	49	56
Fundamentalist Conservative	22	21	15	18	19
Self-Identified Fundamentalist	12	10	6	6	8
Total	99%	100%	99%	100%	101%
(Number of Cases)	(49)	(144)	(130)	(164)	(487)

Theological party	INCOME (Laity)				
	Less than $10,000	$10,000–19,999	$20,000–34,999	$35,000–49,999	$50,000 or more	Average
Self-Identified Moderate	2%	8%	7%	7%	21%	8%
Moderate Conservative	0	3	7	13	14	7
Conservative	61	62	55	54	49	57
Fundamentalist Conservative	23	18	24	15	14	20
Self-Identified Fundamentalist	14	9	8	11	3	9
Total	100%	100%	101%	100%	101%	101%
(Number of Cases)	(64)	(140)	(203)	(100)	(70)	(576)

Theological Party	CHURCH SIZE AND LOCATION (Clergy)				
	Small Rural	Large Rural	Small Urban	Large Urban	Average
Self-Identified Moderate	15%	11%	3%	17%	13%
Moderate Conservative	9	12	15	17	13
Conservative	33	42	41	38	38
Fundamentalist Conservative	30	30	21	21	26
Self-Identified Fundamentalist	13	5	20	7	11
Total	100%	100%	100%	100%	101%
(Number of Cases)	(128)	(74)	(61)	(142)	(405)

Note: All differences between categories are statistically significant at p < .01. Some percentages do not total 100 due to rounding.

have looked even more moderate than they did. Secondly, very few pastors of churches more than 300 in membership were willing to wear the fundamentalist label. If church size was a measure of a pastor's status, then status and fundamentalist identity were negatively related. Those who were more "successful" (as measured by church size) were less likely to be fundamentalist in theology and considerably less likely to claim that identity.

The relationship between church size, status, and theological positions can be seen even more clearly if city churches are looked at separately from country and small town churches (see the bottom section of table 1). A small church is "normal" in a rural or small town setting. In 1985 three-fourths of all rural and small town SBC churches had total memberships under 300. And indeed, size seemed to make little difference among rural pastors. The contrast between small and large churches was much more dramatic among the urban pastors. Barely more than one third (37 percent) of all SBC city churches had memberships under 300. Therefore, pastoring a small church in an urban area was less "normal." In an urban setting, one's neighbors were large, even huge, churches. Pastoring such a small urban church may have engendered a good deal more status anxiety than pastoring the same size church in the country. Similarly, pastoring a large urban church may have carried a good deal more weight than pastoring a large rural one.

Pastors of different size urban churches occupied very different positions in the denomination, then, and indeed those positions were reflected in theological identifications. Pastors of small urban churches were almost three times as likely (20 percent versus 7 percent) to identify themselves as fundamentalist, when compared to pastors of large urban churches. And at the other extreme, large church pastors were over five times as likely (17 percent versus 3 percent) to be self identified moderates compared to their small-church neighbors. Indeed, almost no pastors of small urban churches called themselves moderate. These party identifications reflected real differences in belief. Forty-one percent of small church pastors fell to the right of center, compared to 28 percent of their counterparts in large churches. Thirty-four percent of large church pastors fell to the left of center, compared to 18 percent of those in small churches. Again, it should be remembered that these differences are actually diminished by the presence of fundamentalist super-church pastors in the large urban category. Without that anomaly, the contrast between pastors of small and large churches might be even greater.

The churches represented on each side of the SBC's division, then, were somewhat different. Both sides drew substantially from the small rural churches that were the backbone of the denomination. Fundamentalists were somewhat more dominated by these small rural churches than were conservatives and moderates, but in each faction, oldline Southern Baptist churches were the most numerous. The biggest difference in the composition of the denomination's two sides was in the distribution of urban churches. Over one third of moderate pastors were in urban churches of substantial size. Almost no moderate pastors were in small city churches. Fundamentalist pastors, on the other hand, were more likely (if they were in a city) to be in a small church than in a large one. The tiny fraction of fundamentalist superstar pastors in super churches formed an ironic contrast to their fellow pastors in churches that were tiny by comparison.

In a number of ways status in the denomination and in society appears to have been related to the positions people were taking in the SBC controversy. Those who had more comfortable lives—from white collar and professional families, with more income, and a professional at the head of the household—were more likely to be found to the left of center in the denomination and to declare themselves moderate. In addition, pastors of larger urban churches (the denomination's plums) were also likely to prefer the moderate side. Those who came from farming and blue collar backgrounds, who had less money, and whose jobs involved them in a more routine sort of work, were more attracted to fundamentalist ways of thinking. Status cannot explain all the differences between the Southern Baptist Convention's left and right wings, but it does appear to explain a good deal.

The result was clear differences in the objective status resources available on each side. On the left wing, half had come from white collar and professional homes and nearly all the laity worked in middle class occupations as adults. Very few had incomes below $20,000, substantially more had household incomes over $35,000. Over a third of the clergy in the moderate camp were from large urban churches; very few were in the unusual position of pastoring small urban churches. On the right wing, nearly a quarter were pastoring small urban churches. Fundamentalist laity were split about equally between white collar or professional households and blue collar or farming ones. But about three quarters of them had grown up in farming and blue collar homes. Less than a quarter of fundamentalists had family incomes over $35,000, and over one third earned under $20,000. On the fundamentalist side, there was a wide range from well off to underprivileged, from high status occupations and pastorates to low. On the moderate side, the scales tipped clearly in the direction of higher status.

Another result was a difference in personal style and appearance that was regular enough to be noticed by our observers. Rank and file moderates (men and women) were likely to wear nicely tailored suits, and the men often wore oxford-cloth, button-down collar shirts. They were rarely ostentatious; they looked, rather, like they were used to dressing for the office, to fit in with other professional people. The clothing of rank and file fundamentalists varied between outfits that looked new for the occasion and simple dresses or shirts and slacks that had been worn often before. Fundamentalist women were much more likely to wear a fancy dress than a suit, and their husbands occasionally had ties that were a little too wide or shirts that did not match the rest of their clothes. There was, of course, no uniformity to such observations, but the coincidences happened often enough to make us suspect that real differences existed between the two groups.

Those visible differences were also reflected in the subjective preferences and lifestyles our respondents reported on their surveys. In the last chapter, we noted that fundamentalists and moderates took very different positions on the propriety of various "forbidden" practices. The greater acceptance of movies, cards, dancing, and even alcohol among moderates can be linked to their middle class positions in society. Cultural and economic resources have a great deal to do with the recreations one chooses. The consumption of "high culture," for instance, is linked to social class position, and there is even evidence that appreciation for music and art may aid in social mobility. It is not surprising then, that the same pattern of differences among these Baptist groups emerges when they are asked about their cultural preferences. Nearly all the moderates said they enjoyed "cultural events, such as symphony concerts," while less than half the self-identified fundamentalists said they did.

The cleavages in Southern Baptist life, then, coincided at least in part with differences between a left wing that was predominantly middle- and upper-middle class, and a right wing that contained many of the denomination's less privileged. The relationship was not perfect, of course. There were many middle- and upper-middle class fundamentalists, and a noticeable minority of less privileged moderates. But Niebuhr was right to point us in the direction of social class as one of the components in the differences between Southern Baptist fundamentalists and their moderate opponents.

QUESTIONS

1. What are the "Baptist battles" to which Nancy Tatom Ammerman refers? Is there a right and a wrong in this conflict?

2. In Ammerman's survey results, what kinds of independent variables seem to explain where people stand on the issues that divide the Baptist population?

REMARRIAGE AS AN INCOMPLETE INSTITUTION

Andrew Cherlin

Andrew Cherlin is one of the leading experts on divorce and remarriage in the United States. As a sociologist of the family he has done a great deal to clarify the confusions that surround controversial social phenomena like divorce. His research on remarriage is extremely important as well. It has contributed to our understanding of the problems people face in second marriages.

Many family researchers focus on divorce and its consequences. The text reviews some of this research, especially that which deals with trends in divorce and with the impact of divorce on children. But Cherlin is also extremely concerned with the changing institutions of family life. He shows in this selection that remarriage is an "incomplete institution" in which the relatively new roles of stepparents are not always well defined in the law or in common practice. As a result of the rise in the number of divorces during this century, the problems encountered in remarriages, especially those that include children from earlier marriages, affect hundreds of thousands of people and deserve greater attention in a society that prides itself on fostering "family values."

Remarriages have been common in the United States since its beginnings, but until this century almost all remarriages followed widowhood. In the Plymouth Colony, for instance, about one-third of all men and one-quarter of all women who lived full lifetimes remarried after the death of a spouse, but there was little divorce (Demos 1970). Even as late as the 1920s, more brides and grooms were remarrying after widowhood than after divorce, according to estimates by Jacobson (1959). Since then, however, a continued increase in divorce (Norton and Glick 1976) has altered this pattern. By 1975, 84% of all brides who were remarrying were previously divorced, and 16% were widowed. For grooms who were remarrying in 1975, 86% were previously divorced (U.S. National Center for Health Statistics 1977). Thus, it is only recently that remarriage after divorce has become the predominant form of remarriage.

And since the turn of the century, remarriages after divorce have increased as a proportion of all marriages. In 1900 only 3% of all brides—including both the single and previously married—were divorced (Jacobson 1959). In 1930, 9% of all brides were divorced (Jacobson 1959), and in 1975, 25% of all brides were divorced (U.S. National Center for Health Statistics 1977). As a result, in 7 million families in 1970 one or both spouses had remarried after a divorce (U.S. Bureau of the Census 1973). Most of this increase is due to the rise in the divorce rate, but some part is due to the greater tendency of divorced and widowed adults to remarry. The remarriage rate for divorced and widowed women was about 50% higher in the mid-1970s than in 1940 (Norton and Glick 1976).

At the same time, the percentage of divorces which involved at least one child increased from 46% in 1950 to 60% in 1974 (U.S. National Center for Health Statistics 1953, 1977). The increase in the percentage of divorces which involve children means that more families of remarriages after divorce now have stepchildren. Although it is not possible with available data to calculate the exact number of families with stepchildren, we do know that in 1970 8.9 million children lived in two-parent families where one or both parents had been previously divorced (U.S. Bureau of the Census 1973). Some of these children—who constituted 15% of all children living in two-parent families—were from previous marriages, and others were from the remarriages.

Can these families of remarriages after divorce, many of which include children from previous marriages, maintain unity as well as do families of first marriages? Not according to the divorce rate. A number of studies have shown a greater risk of separation and divorce for remarriages after divorce (Becker, Landes, and Michael 1976; Bumpass and Sweet 1972; Cherlin 1977; Monahan 1958). Remarriages after widowhood appear, in contrast, to have a lower divorce rate than first marriages (Monahan 1958). A recent Bureau of the Census report (U.S. Bureau of the Census 1976) estimated that about 33% of all first marriages among people 25–35 may end in divorce, while about 40% of remarriages after divorce among people this age may end in divorce. The estimates are based on current rates of divorce, which could, of course, change greatly in the future.

Conventional wisdom, however, seems to be that remarriages are more successful than first marriages. In a small, nonrandom sample of family counselors and remarried couples, I found most to be surprised at the news that divorce was more prevalent in remarriages. There are some plausible reasons for this popular misconception. Those who remarry are older, on the average, than those marrying for the first time and are presumably more mature. They have had more time to search the marriage market and to determine their own needs and preferences. In addition, divorced men may be in a better financial position and command greater work skills than younger, never-married men. (Divorced women who are supporting children, however, are often in a worse financial position—see Hoffman [1977].)

But despite these advantages, the divorce rate is higher in remarriages after divorce. The reported differences are often modest, but they appear consistently throughout 20 years of research. And the meaning of marital dissolution for family unity is clear: when a marriage dissolves, unity ends. The converse, though, is not necessarily true: a family may have a low degree of unity but remain nominally intact. Even with this limitation, I submit that the divorce rate is the best objective indicator of differences in family unity between remarriages and first marriages.

There are indicators of family unity other than divorce, but their meaning is less clear and their measurement is more difficult. There is the survey research tradition, for example, of asking people how happy or satisfied they are with their marriages. The invariable result is that almost everyone reports that they are very happy. (See, e.g., Bradburn and Caplovitz 1965; Campbell, Converse, and Rodgers 1976; Glenn 1975.) It may be that our high rate of divorce increases the general level of marital satisfaction by dissolving unsatisfactory marriages. But it is also possible that the satisfaction ratings are inflated by the reluctance of some respondents to admit that their marriages are less than fully satisfying. Marriage is an important part of life for most adults—the respondents in the Campbell et al. (1976) national sample rated it second only to health as the most important aspect of their lives—and people may be reluctant to admit publicly that their marriage is troubled.

Several recent studies, nevertheless, have shown that levels of satisfaction and happiness are lower among the remarried, although the differences typically are small. Besides the Campbell et al. study, these include Glenn and Weaver (1977), who found modest differences in marital happiness in the 1973, 1974, and 1975 General Social Surveys conducted by the National Opinion Research Center. They reported that for women, the difference between those who were remarried and those who were in a first marriage was statistically significant, while for men the difference was smaller and not significant. In addition, Renne (1971) reported that remarried, previously divorced persons were less happy with their marriages than those in first marriages in a probability sample of 4,452 Alameda County, California, households. Again, the differences were modest, but they were consistent within categories of age, sex, and race. No tests of significance were reported.

The higher divorce rate suggests that maintaining family unity is more difficult for families of remarriages after divorce. And the lower levels of marital satisfaction, which must be interpreted cautiously, also support this hypothesis. It is true, nevertheless, that many remarriages work well, and that the majority of remarriages will not end in divorce. And we must remember that the divorce rate is also at an all-time high for first marriages. But there is a difference of degree between remarriages and first marriages which appears consistently in research. We must ask why families of remarriages after divorce seem to have more difficulty maintaining family unity than do families of first marriages. Several explanations have been proposed, and we will now assess the available evidence for each.

PREVIOUS EXPLANATIONS

One explanation, favored until recently by many psychiatrists, is that the problems of remarried people arise from personality disorders which preceded their marriages (see Bergler 1948). People in troubled marriages, according to this view, have unresolved personal conflicts which must be treated before a successful marriage can be achieved. Their problems lead them to marry second spouses who may be superficially quite different from their first spouse but are characterologically quite similar. As a result, this theory states, remarried people repeat the problems of their first marriages.

If this explanation were correct, one would expect that people in remarriages would show higher levels of psychiatric symptomatology than people in first marriages. But there is little evidence of this. On the contrary, Overall (1971) reported that in a sample of 2,000 clients seeking help for psychiatric problems, currently remarried people showed lower levels of psychopathology on a general rating scale than persons in first marriages and currently divorced persons. These findings, of course, apply only to people who sought psychiatric help. And it may be, as Overall noted, that the differences emerged because remarried people are more likely to seek help for less serious problems. The findings, nevertheless, weaken the psychoanalytic interpretation of the problems of remarried life.

On the other hand, Monahan (1958) and Cherlin (1977) reported that the divorce rate was considerably higher for people in their third marriages who had divorced twice than for people in their second marriages. Perhaps personality disorders among some of those who marry several times prevent them from achieving a successful marriage. But even with the currently high rates of divorce and remarriage, only a small proportion of all adults marry more than twice. About 10% of all adults in 1975 had married twice, but less than 2% had married three or more times (U.S. Bureau of the Census 1976).

Most remarried people, then, are in a second marriage. And the large number of people now divorcing and entering a second marriage also undercuts the psychoanalytic interpretation. If current rates hold, about one-third of all young married people will become divorced, and about four-fifths of these will remarry. It is hard to believe that the recent increases in divorce and remarriage are due to the sudden spread of marriage-threatening personality disorders to a large part of the young adult population. I conclude, instead, that the psychoanalytic explanation for the rise in divorce and the difficulties of remarried spouses and their children is at best incomplete.[1]

A second possible explanation is that once a person has divorced he or she is less hesitant to do so again. Having divorced once, a person knows how to get divorced and what to expect from family members, friends, and the courts. This explanation is plausible and probably accounts for some of the difference in divorce rates. But it does not account for all of the research findings on remarriage, such as the finding of Becker et al. (1976) that the presence of children from a previous marriage increased the probability of divorce for women in remarriages, while the presence of children from the new marriage reduced the probability of divorce. I will discuss the implications of this study below, but let me note here that a general decrease in the reluctance of remarried persons to divorce would not explain this finding. Moreover, the previously divorced may be more hesitant to divorce again because of the stigma attached to divorcing twice. Several remarried people I interviewed expressed great reluctance to divorce a second time. They reasoned that friends and relatives excused one divorce but would judge them incompetent at marriage after two divorces.

Yet another explanation for the higher divorce rate is the belief that many remarried men are deficient at fulfilling their economic responsibilities. We know that divorce is more likely in families where the husband has low earnings (Goode 1956). Some remarried men, therefore, may be unable to earn a sufficient amount of money to support a family. It is conceivable that this inability to be a successful breadwinner could account for all of the divorce rate differential, but statistical studies of divorce suggest otherwise. Three recent multivariate analyses of survey data on divorce have shown that remarried persons still had a higher probability of divorce

[1]Despite the lack of convincing evidence, I am reluctant to discount this explanation completely. Clinical psychologists and psychiatrists with whom I have talked insist that many troubled married persons they have treated had made the same mistakes twice and were in need of therapy to resolve long-standing problems. Their clinical experience should not be ignored, but this "divorce-proneness" syndrome seems inadequate as a complete explanation for the greater problems of remarried people.

or separation, independent of controls for such socioeconomic variables as husband's earnings (Becker et al. 1976), husband's educational attainment (Bumpass and Sweet 1972), and husband's and wife's earnings, employment status, and savings (Cherlin 1977). These analyses show that controlling for low earnings can reduce the difference in divorce probabilities, but they also show that low earnings cannot fully explain the difference. It is possible, nevertheless, that a given amount of income must be spread thinner in many remarriages, because of child-support or alimony payments (although the remarried couple also may be receiving these payments). But this type of financial strain must be distinguished from the questionable notion that many remarried husbands are inherently unable to provide for a wife and children.

INSTITUTIONAL SUPPORT

The unsatisfactory nature of all these explanations leads us to consider one more interpretation. I hypothesize that the difficulties of couples in remarriages after divorce stem from a lack of institutionalized guidelines for solving many common problems of their remarried life. The lack of institutional support is less serious when neither spouse has a child from a previous marriage. In this case, the family of remarriage closely resembles families of first marriages, and most of the norms for first marriages apply. But when at least one spouse has children from a previous marriage, family life often differs sharply from first marriages. Frequently, as I will show, family members face problems quite unlike those in first marriages—problems for which institutionalized solutions do not exist. And without accepted solutions to their problems, families of remarriages must resolve difficult issues by themselves. As a result, solving everyday problems is sometimes impossible without engendering conflict and confusion among family members.

The complex structure of families of remarriages after divorce which include children from a previous marriage has been noted by others (Bernard 1956; Bohannan 1970; Duberman 1975). These families are expanded in the number of social roles and relationships they possess and also are expanded in space over more than one household. The additional social roles include stepparents, stepchildren, stepsiblings, and the new spouses of noncustodial parents, among others. And the links between the households are the children of previous marriages. These children are commonly in the custody of one parent—usually the mother—but they normally visit the noncustodial parent regularly. Thus they promote communication among the divorced parents, the new stepparent, and the noncustodial parent's new spouse.

Family relationships can be quite complex, because the new kin in a remarriage after divorce do not, in general, replace the kin from the first marriage as they do in a remarriage after widowhood. Rather, they add to the existing kin (Fast and Cain 1966). But this complexity alone does not necessarily imply that problems of family unity will develop. While families of remarriages may appear complicated to Americans, there are many societies in which complicated kinship rules and family patterns coexist with a functioning, stable family system (Bohannan, 1963; Fox 1967).

In most of these societies, however, familial roles and relationships are well defined. Family life may seem complex to Westerners, but activity is regulated by established patterns of behavior. The central difference, then, between families of remarriages in the United States and complicated family situations in other societies is the lack of institutionalized social regulation of remarried life in this country. Our society, oriented toward first marriages, provides little guidance on problems peculiar to remarriages, especially remarriages after divorce.

In order to illustrate the incomplete institutionalization of remarriage and its consequences for family life, let us examine two of the major institutions in society: language and the law. "Language," Gerth and Mills (1953, p. 305) wrote, "is necessary to the operations of institutions. For the symbols used in institutions coordinate the roles that compose them, and justify the enactment of these roles by the members of the institution." Where no adequate terms exist for an important social role, the institutional support for this role is deficient, and general acceptance of the role as a legitimate pattern of activity is questionable.

Consider English terms for the roles peculiar to remarriage after divorce. The term "stepparent," as Bohannan (1970) has observed, originally meant a person who replaced a dead parent, not a person who was an additional parent. And the negative connotations of the "stepparent," especially the "stepmother," are well known (Bernard 1956; Smith 1953). Yet there are no other terms in use. In some situations, no term exists for a child to use in addressing a stepparent. If the child calls her mother "mom," for example, what should she call her stepmother? This lack of appropriate terms for parents in remarriages after divorce can have negative consequences for family functioning. In one family I interviewed, the wife's children wanted to call their stepfather "dad," but the stepfather's own children, who also lived in the household, refused to allow this usage. To them, sharing the term "dad" represented a threat to their claim on their father's attention and affection. The dispute caused bad feelings, and it impaired the father's ability to act as a parent to all the children in the household.

For more extended relationships, the lack of appropriate terms is even more acute. At least the word "step-parent," however inadequate, has a widely accepted meaning. But there is no term a child living with his mother can use to describe his relationship to the woman his father remarried after he divorced the child's mother. And, not surprisingly, the rights and duties of the child and this woman toward each other are unclear. Nor is the problem limited to kinship terms. Suppose a child's parents both remarry and he alternates between their households under a joint custody arrangement. Where, then, is his "home"? And who are the members of his "family"? These linguistic inadequacies correspond to the absence of widely accepted definitions for many of the roles and relationships in families of remarriage. The absence of proper terms is both a symptom and a cause of some of the problems of remarried life.

As for the law, it is both a means of social control and an indicator of accepted patterns of behavior. It was to the law, for instance, that Durkheim turned for evidence on the forms of social solidarity. When we examine family law, we find a set of traditional guidelines, based on precedent, which define the rights and duties of family members. But as Weitzman (1974) has shown, implicit in the precedents is the assumption that the marriage in question is a first marriage. For example, Weitzman found no provisions for several problems of re-marriage, such as balancing the financial obligations of husbands to their spouses and children from current and previous marriages, defining the wife's obligations to husbands and children from the new and the old marriages, and reconciling the competing claims of current and ex-spouses for shares of the estate of a deceased spouse.

Legal regulations concerning incest and consanguineal marriage are also inadequate for families of remar-riages. In all states marriage and sexual relations are prohibited between persons closely related by blood, but in many states these restrictions do not cover sexual relations or marriage between other family members in a remarriage—between a stepmother and a stepson, for example, or between two stepchildren (Goldstein and Katz 1965). Mead (1970), among others, has argued that incest taboos serve the important function of allowing children to develop affection for and identification with other family members without the risk of sexual ex-ploitation. She suggested that current beliefs about incest—as embodied in law and social norms—fail to pro-vide adequate security and protection for children in households of remarriage.

The law, then, ignores the special problems of families of remarriages after divorce. It assumes, for the most part, that remarriages are similar to first marriages. Families of remarriages after divorce, consequently, often must deal with problems such as financial obligations or sexual relations without legal regulations or clear legal precedent. The law, like the language, offers incomplete institutional support to families of remarriages.

In addition, other customs and conventions of family life are deficient when applied to remarriages after divorce. Stepparents, for example, have difficulty determining their proper disciplinary relationship to stepchil-dren. One woman I interviewed, determined not to show favoritism toward her own children, disciplined them more harshly than her stepchildren. Other couples who had children from the wife's previous marriage reported that the stepfather had difficulty establishing himself as a disciplinarian in the household. Fast and Cain (1966), in a study of about 50 case records from child-guidance settings, noted many uncertainties among step-parents about appropriate role behavior. They theorized that the uncertainties derived from the sharing of the role of parent between the stepparent and the noncustodial, biological parent. Years ago, when most remar-riages took place after widowhood, this sharing did not exist. Now, even though most remarriages follow di-vorce, generally accepted guidelines for sharing parenthood still have not emerged.

There is other evidence consistent with the idea that the incomplete institutionalization of remarriage after divorce may underlie the difficulties of families of remarriages. Becker et al. (1976) analyzed the Survey of Economic Opportunity, a nationwide study of approximately 30,000 households. As I mentioned above, they found that the presence of children from a previous marriage increased the probability of divorce for women in remarriages, while the presence of children from the new marriage reduced the probability of divorce. This is as we would expect, since children from a previous marriage expand the family across households and complicate the structure of family roles and relationships. But children born into the new marriage bring none of these complications. Consequently, only children from a previous marriage should add to the special problems of families of remarriages[2].

In addition, Goetting (1978a, 1978b) studied the attitudes of remarried people toward relationships among adults who are associated by broken marital ties, such as ex-spouses and the people ex-spouses remarry. Bohannan (1970) has called these people "quasi-kin." Goetting presented hypothetical situations involving the behavior of quasi-kin to 90 remarried men and 90 remarried women who were white, previously divorced, and who had children from previous marriages. The subjects were asked to approve, disapprove, or express indifference about the behavior in each situation. Goetting then arbitrarily decided that the respondents reached "consensus" on a given situation if any of the three possible response categories received more than half of all responses. But even by this lenient definition, consensus was not reached on the proper behavior in most of the hypothetical situations. For example, in situations involving conversations between a person's present spouse and his or her ex-spouse, the only consensus of the respondents was that the pair should say "hello." Beyond that, there was no consensus on whether they should engage in polite conversation in public places or on the telephone or whether the ex-spouse should be invited into the new spouse's home while waiting to pick up his or her children. Since meetings of various quasi-kin must occur regularly in the lives of most respondents, their disagreement is indicative of their own confusion about how to act in common family situations.

Still, there are many aspects of remarried life which are similar to life in first marriages, and these are subject to established rules of behavior. Even some of the unique aspects of remarriage may be regulated by social norms—such as the norms concerning the size and nature of wedding ceremonies in remarriages (Hollingshead 1952). Furthermore, as Goode (1956) noted, remarriage is itself an institutional solution to the ambiguous status of the divorced (and not remarried) parent. But the day-to-day life of remarried adults and their children also includes many problems for which there are no institutionalized solutions. And since members of a household of remarriage often have competing or conflicting interests (Bernard 1956), the lack of consensual solutions can make these problems more serious than they otherwise would be. One anthropologist, noting the lack of relevant social norms, wrote, "the present situation approaches chaos, with each individual set of families having to work out its own destiny without any realistic guidelines" (Bohannan 1970, p. 137).

REFERENCES

Becker, G., E. Landes, and R. Michael. 1976. "Economics of Marital Instability." Working Paper no. 153. Stanford, Calif.: National Bureau of Economic Research.

Bergler, Edmund. 1948. *Divorce Won't Help.* New York: Harper & Bros.

Bernard, Jessie. 1956. *Remarriage.* New York: Dryden.

Bohannan, Paul. 1963. *Social Anthropology.* New York: Holt, Rinehart and Winston.

———. 1970. "Divorce Chains, Households of Remarriage, and Multiple Divorces." Pp. 127–39 in *Divorce and After,* edited by Paul Bohannan. New York: Doubleday.

Bradburn, Norman, and David Caplovitz. 1965. *Reports on Happiness.* Chicago: Aldine.

Bumpass, L. L., and A. Sweet. 1972. "Differentials in Marital Instability: 1970." *American Sociological Review* 37 (December): 754–66.

[2]In an earlier paper (Cherlin 1977), I found that children affected the probability that a woman in a first marriage or remarriage would divorce only when the children were of preschool age. But the National Longitudinal Surveys of Mature Women, from which this analysis was drawn, contained no information about whether the children of remarried wives were from the woman's previous or current marriage. Since the Becker et al. (1976) results showed that this distinction is crucial, we cannot draw any relevant inferences about children and remarriage from my earlier study.

Campbell, Angus, Philip E. Converse, and Willard L. Rodgers. 1976. *The Quality of American Life.* New York: Russell Sage.

Cherlin, A. 1977. "The Effects of Children on Marital Dissolution." *Demography* 14 (August): 265–72.

Demos, John. 1970. *A Little Commonwealth: Family Life in Plymouth Colony.* New York: Oxford University Press.

Duberman, Lucile. 1975. *The Reconstituted Family.* Chicago: Nelson-Hall.

Fast, I., and A. C. Cain. 1966. "The Stepparent Role: Potential for Disturbances in Family Functioning." *American Journal of Orthopsychiatry* 36 (April): 485–91.

Fox, Robin. 1967. *Kinship and Marriage.* Baltimore: Penguin.

Gerth, Hans, and C. Wright Mills. 1953. *Character and Social Structure.* New York: Harcourt Brace & Co.

Glenn, N. 1975. "The Contribution of Marriage to the Psychological Well-Being of Males and Females." *Journal of Marriage and the Family* 37 (August): 594–601.

Glenn, N., and C. Weaver. 1977. "The Marital Happiness of Remarried Divorced Persons." *Journal of Marriage and the Family* 39 (May):331–37.

Goetting, Ann. 1978a. "The Normative Integration of the Former Spouse Relationship." Paper presented at the annual meeting of the American Sociological Association, San Francisco, September 4–8.

———. 1978b. "The Normative Integration of Two Divorce Chain Relationships." Paper presented at the annual meeting of the Southwestern Sociological Association, Houston, April 12–15.

Goldstein, Joseph, and Jay Katz. 1965. *The Family and the Law.* New York: Free Press.

Goode, William J. 1956. *Women in Divorce.* New York: Free Press.

Hoffman, S. 1977. "Marital Instability and the Economic Status of Women." *Demography* 14 (February): 67–76.

Hollingshead, A. B. 1952. "Marital Status and Wedding Behavior." *Marriage and Family Living* (November), pp. 308–11.

Jacobson, Paul H. 1959. *American Marriage and Divorce.* New York: Rinehart.

Mead, M. 1970. "Anomalies in American Postdivorce Relationships." Pp. 107–25 in *Divorce and After,* edited by Paul Bohannan. New York: Doubleday.

Monahan, T. P. 1958. "The Changing Nature and Instability of Remarriages." *Eugenics Quarterly* 5: 73–85.

Norton, A. J., and P. C. Glick. 1976. "Marital Instability; Past, Present, and Future." *Journal of Social Issues* 32 (Winter): 5.

Overall, J. E. 1971. "Associations between Marital History and the Nature of Manifest Psychopathology." *Journal of Abnormal Psychology* 78 (2): 213–21.

Renne, K. S. 1971. "Health and Marital Experience in an Urban Population." *Journal of Marriage and the Family* 33 (May): 338–50.

Smith, William C. 1953. *The Stepchild.* Chicago: University of Chicago Press.

U.S. Bureau of Census. 1973. *U.S. Census of the Population: 1970. Persons by Family Characteristics.* Final Report PC(2)-4B. Washington, D.C.: Government Printing Office.

———. 1976. *Number, Timing, and Duration of Marriages and Divorces in the United States: June 1975.* Current Population Reports, Series P-20, No. 297. Washington, D.C.: Government Printing Office.

U.S. National Center for Health Statistics. 1953. *Vital Statistics of the United States, 1950.* Vol. 2. *Marriage, Divorce, Natality, Fetal Mortality, and Infant Mortality Data.* Washington, D.C.: Government Printing Office.

———. 1977. *Vital Statistics Report. Advance Report. Final Marriage Statistics, 1975.* Washington, D.C.: Government Printing Office.

Weitzman, L. J. 1974. "Legal Regulation of Marriage: Tradition and Change." *California Law Review* 62:1169–1288.

QUESTIONS

1. According to Andrew Cherlin, what are some of the complications encountered by people in second marriages?

2. What does Cherlin mean when he says that remarriage is an incomplete institution?

CREDITS AND ACKNOWLEDGMENTS

Ammerman, Nancy Tatom. "Differences in Social Status" from *Baptist Battles: Social Change and Religious Conflict in the Southern Baptist Convention*. Copyright © 1990 by Nancy Tatom Ammerman. Reprinted by permission of Rutgers University Press.

Cherlin, Andrew. "Remarriage as an Incomplete Institution" from *American Journal of Sociology*, Volume 84, number 3. Copyright © 1978 by University of Chicago Press.

Epstein, Cynthia Fuchs. "The Structure of Work and the Economic Pyramid" from *Deceptive Distinctions*. Copyright © 1988 by Yale University.

Goffman, Erving. "Stigma and Social Identity" from *Stigma: Notes on Management of Spoiled Identity*. Copyright © 1963 by Prentice-Hall, Inc., renewed 1991. Reprinted with the permission of Simon & Schuster.

Jussawalla, Feroza. Excerpts from *Writing in the Disciplines*, Third Edition. Copyright © 1995 by Harcourt Brace & Company. Reprinted by permission of the publisher.

Mills, C. Wright. "The Corporate Rich" from *The Power Elite*. Copyright © 1959 by C. Wright Mills. Used by permission of Oxford University Press, Inc.

Orwell, George. "Politics and the English Language" from *Shooting an Elephant and Other Essays*. Copyright © 1946 by Sonia Brownell Orwell and renewed 1974 by Sonia Orwell. Reprinted by permission of Harcourt Brace and Company.

Portes, Alejandro and Rumbaut, Rubén G. "Who They Are and Why They Come" from *Immigrant America*. Copyright © 1990 by University of California Press. Reprinted by permission.

Sterk, Claire. "Prostitutes, Drug Users and AIDS" from *In the Field: Readings on the Field Research Experience, 2e*. Copyright © 1996 by Praeger Books. Reproduced with permission of Greenwood Publishing Group, Inc., Westport, CT.

Townsend, Peter. "The Changing World Map of Poverty" from *The International Analysis of Poverty*. Copyright © 1993 Harvester Wheatsheaf.